KALEIDOSCOPE OF COLORS II

"Each poem will take you on a different path, whether it be vulnerability, loss, love, friendships, or powerful memories. All of these messages converge to create a beautiful representation of the human experience."
> —Holland Parker, *Reedsy Discovery* on *kaleidoscope of colors*

"His ability to reproduce the sights and sounds of the natural world in his readers' minds is rather superb...Cozzi is not a poet who is afraid of the work which comes with writing...his nature poems are without a doubt, fantastic reading material."
> —*Berry's Poetry Book Reviews* on *kaleidoscope of colors*

"Robert A. Cozzi has written about romance, memories, loneliness, as well as hope."
> —Virendra Soni on *Perspective to Pen: An Anthology*

"Robert Cozzi has a knack for creating sharp emotional textures..."
> —BookView Review on *Perspective to Pen: An Anthology*

"Robert A. Cozzi...[has written]...pieces that are timely...as well as looking with nostalgia on the past and hope for the future."
> —*Self-Publishing Review* on *Perspective to Pen: An Anthology*

WORKS BY ROBERT A. COZZI:

tide pool of words (2013)
Handful of Memories (2014)
Blanket of Hearts (2016)
Sky of Dreams (2017)
kaleidoscope of colors (2019)
kaleidoscope of colors II (2021)
Two Kinds of Love (2021)*

ANTHOLOGIES:

Social Distances (2020)
Perspective to Pen: An Anthology (2020)

*Denotes forthcoming book

CONTENTS

--

FOREWORD

I first met Robert A. Cozzi in 2019 in the beautiful world that is the Instagram poetry community. At the time, I was a new poet still writing under a pseudonym and shocked that an award-winning poet would reach out to me asking for more of my work. But that's Robert: a friend and mentor to all creatives. We exchanged our published books and our intimate stories and, in the process, forged a friendship that is poetry itself.

From the very first word of his poems to cross my lips to the advanced copy of this manuscript at my side, Robert whisks me away like Alice to his Wonderland. His work deliciously teases all six senses and takes the reader on an emotional technicolor exploration of the human experience. I still wonder how he manages to deftly describe the duality of my deepest pain alongside a never-ending joy and wonder at the beauty that surrounds me as if he's been reading my private journal entries.

kaleidoscope of colors II continues where the first left off, an ever-changing pattern of imagery and emotion in prose and poetry that flow together seamlessly with each turn of the page. If you're new to Robert's work, I beg you to read each piece aloud. That is the best way to savor the flavor of the words on your tongue. Pause to breathe in the ocean air on Folly Beach and feel the gritty Jersey shore sand between your toes.

Let the drumbeat overtake you as your heart syncs up in joy, grief, missed opportunities, desire, unwavering hope, and a relentless belief in love and humanity.

Enjoy the journey.
-Lisa Bain

This book is dedicated to:

Charanjit Randhawa, my second father; you are missed every day
Gurdeep Randhawa, my second mother
Mom, Dad, and Annmarie
Ben, Jairo, and Evan, my Bard Brothers
Kai, my best friend

"Write in recollection and amazement for yourself."
-Jack Kerouac

KALEIDOSCOPE

OF

COLORS

II

The Sound Heard Above the City

It takes a moment for you

To look up from the book you are reading

You are seated at a small, stained-glass table

In this intimate outdoor café

An array of emotion fills your face

Before you stand up with your inherent grace

You still have a swimmer's build

But your eyes are not as blue

They seem to have faded gently, like a memory

Your hair is no longer tousled and bleached from the sun

It has matured into a darker, more conservative-looking blond

When you come to me, we embrace

A grimace of happiness cracks my mouth

As a veil of your aroma envelops me

Bringing back the feeling, not just the memory

Of the years we spent together

Inside the embrace, I can feel the sand of Folly Beach

And smell the ocean air and remember what it was like

To be so completely loved by you

But once you pull away

I hear my heart crack above the sounds of the city

Midnight Swim

Take off your clothes
Swim with me
Beneath the dying stars

Let's get lost
In this hurricane
Of forgotten inhibitions

The Tide Never Stops

Some days it is bearable

Some days it burns

Grief is a lot like the Atlantic Ocean

It moves in ebbs and flows

Often turbulent and rough

Or peaceful and settled

And even over time

When you learn to sail across its waters

The tide never stops

Kissed by the Sea

The swirling mist
From the sea
Provides a refreshing caress
As it masterfully
Sculpts rainbows
Into a breathless sky

The First Time I Saw You

I remember the first time
I saw you at the beach
You and Tugger were playing Frisbee
I was sitting in a secluded area
Writing in my journal

After watching the two of you for a while
I wrote something about
How you can tell a lot about a person
By how they treat children and animals

When a little girl playing nearby
Suddenly had a nosebleed and panicked
You were next to her like a shot
You pulled a blue bandana from around your neck
Putting your hand on the back of the girl's head
And the bandana to her face
Sitting her down gently on the sand
Speaking to her quietly
As the girl's parents rushed over

I thought
There it is
The bright flag of your disposition
How you give things to others
Without needing to stop and think

Everything goes straight from your heart
To your hands

I knew that day
That I wanted you
In my life

His Art

A drop of sorrow

Twists his heart

Pulling ink from his pen

And once the feelings are written

The atmosphere is lighter

Because those words on the page

Have become his art

Medley of Butterflies

A medley of butterflies

Written in pitch-black ink

Come to life in crystalline beauty

Fluttering along swirling winds

Sharing light with the lonely lighthouse below

As crashing waves sing from the sea

Happy to Be with You

The air is sweet with roasted peanuts
I don't see you at first
Because the area around the fountain is packed with people
Children are running all around the fountain's edge
Zigzagging past their parents
Shrieking out loud each time the water sprays onto their clothes
But then I see you
You are hoisted up on the base of one of the lampposts
Scanning the crowd
I wave in your direction
Your face brightens when you see me
Your shiny black hair is long and hangs in your eyes
You aren't obviously beautiful
But you're beautiful
It is a combination of charm and intelligence
A kind of earthy old-world grace
That makes me happy
Just to be with you
Even if we aren't anything
More than friends

The End of Us

It was just three weeks earlier
That we sat across from one another
At my kitchen table
I knew something was off
Because I read your body language
After eight cumulative years together
It is not so difficult reading such things
I noticed the bead of sweat dancing on your cheek
You took a swig of your black coffee
Before exhaling
I remember hearing you say that you were sorry
That you no longer loved me
And that was when I stopped listening

I hadn't seen this coming
And immediately began to rewind
Looking for signs of your discontent
But I found no answers

I must have been staring off into space for a few minutes
Because when I felt your hand turn my face back to yours

You were sitting beside me
Asking me to let you explain
I listened until you told me
That you had met someone else

I got up and paced back and forth
My heart pounding in my chest
As I felt the ache spread across my shoulders
Down my arms and legs

I forgot how to breathe

Until you raised your voice
Trying hard to earn my attention back
However, it was too late for that
I had heard enough
In a whisper, I asked you to leave
You hesitated before making a move to the door
Stopping to give me a hug first
Which I didn't return

I watched you walk out and get into your car
You didn't look back

Yellow Through the Grey

After we escape the torrential storm
I stand next to you inside Dunkin' Donuts
Sipping my hot chocolate
Admiring how beautiful the rain looks
Bouncing off the horizontal roof outside
Noticing how the light from the window
Has cast raindrop shadows across your face

Even though it is dark grey out there
Your presence here next to me
Reminds me of the bright yellow light
Of daybreak

Could It Be?

When hearts are shattered beyond repair
They are not supposed to beat again
So why does my chest get all tight when I see you?
Why does my pulse race when I think
About holding your hand and kissing your lips?
Could it be that you have somehow upended
My comfortably numb existence?

Disingenuous

When your words land
They're like small drops of rainwater
Striking a windowpane
Each word a little impact
A soft hollow sound
Empty

The Aftermath of Us

At Alicia's party
I am already tired of talking about our breakup
When I see you walk in

I should have made a move to leave
But I stand in place
Watching you smile and greet everyone
Even now
I think I could write a novel about how attractive you are
Which makes me realize that you are a need that can't be satiated

When we find each other
We settle into our familiar place of uncertainty
Lost in a question-filled stare-down

Heat grows on my skin
When your gaze falls to my lips
I freeze
Torn between backing away and leaning in
"I can't do this," I say out loud
Before walking to the door faster than I intend

My pace matches my heartbeat
As I fight to regain some semblance of control
When I look back
You stare at me with confusion and question
Until you wipe the conflict from your face
And shift your focus back to the party
The weeks and months that follow all get easier
Even after all these years
Twelve to be exact
Your mom still calls me on my birthday
The pain I felt back then has long since faded
Because I can smile now when she mentions you

I Wrote It All for You

Seven years ago
Back when you still looked at me
With eyes that ignored everyone else
I wrote it all for you
In a tide pool of words

Sometimes I wish
You would miss me
But I suppose
You're someone else's poetry now

Rebecca

My favorite photo of you
Was taken by Eliot
Outside The Limelight on West 20th Street

In it
People can be seen behind you in the dark
But you're the only one looking at the camera
The glare of the flash is bright on your skin
You appear gripped by joy
With your eyes closed
And your mouth stretched impossibly wide
Revealing teeth that are large and imperfect
An upper one in front is ever so slightly skewed

The very first time I saw it
I knew I wanted to be smiled at like that

New York Supermoon

Under the supermoon
We stroll upon our silhouettes
Two spirits swaying in the summer wind
Painting moonlight with every step

Wading in the Water with You

Once the tide starts coming in
I duck my head under one last time
Before swimming back to shore
When I look up and wipe my eyes
I find you standing at the water's edge
Taking photographs of me

I am not sure what to do
I just stand there, regarding you
Watching as you lower your camera
Your eyes bright even at this distance

Prismatic layers of light
Glint off the water
Like a kaleidoscope
Shattering the sunlight
Into myriad renderings
As you sling your camera
Around your neck
Wading in to join me

I swallow hard
Feeling your soft breath
Up against my neck
My eyes stare into yours
Until our lips meet gently
Then with force

Whitman at 3 a.m.

It's 3 a.m.
I cannot get back to sleep
So I pick up my book of Walt Whitman poems
And begin to read *Song of Myself*
A massive poem
Written when the country
Was at war with itself
Absolutely broken
In it he paints an image of America
Anyone can buy into

As I read
I am swept up in his words
I always am
It is what I love most about him
The feelings he arouses

I especially love the section
Where he names people
He wants to include everyone
He wants to find a place for everyone
An equal place
A place in his affection too

There are those wonderful moments
He puts in parentheses
Like a whisper
Where he tells us he loves
The person he has just named
This is what he thought democracy was
A poem that said these things out loud
Making an occasion for us to love them

I believe that he wanted

To stitch America up
Break all the divisions down

In Whitman's America
People must come together
Without losing their ability to think
Whitman calls it a "thoughtful merge"

His image of America
Still feels like something
I want to buy into
It still feels
Like the best image
Of ourselves

Ocean Vibes

The lifespan
Of this blue-green ocean wave
Incandescent under the sunlight
Making its way to shore
Is akin to two
Uninterrupted
Heartbeats

Watermelon Wishes

I wish things were different
I wish you weren't such a wildcard
I wish I could kiss those perfect lips of yours
One more time without the regret
I wish you would stop squinting at me on FaceTime
I wish you weren't so bloody engaging
I wish that each time I thought of you
I didn't see myself
Unbuttoning you slowly, kissing your collarbone
I wish you didn't remind me
Of watermelon in summer explored down to the rind
I wish I could stop writing about you
I wish I didn't want you back

A Little Sigh of Happiness

You're late
You're always late
Thirty minutes pass by
Before I spot you
Bounding through the front door

You see me right away

Without waiting to be greeted by a server
You make your way over
Pulling off your hat and scarf as you walk

As I watch
I am struck again by your beauty
Which is offhanded and accidental
With your tousled hair and laid-back style

Yours is a beauty stripped of self-regard
And when we hug hello
I hear you make the sound I have come to love
A little sigh of happiness
And all my irritation
Simply drains away

Transformation at the Diner

I watch as you turn your face
To the glass beside us
Watching the rain
Already, the last of the light is fading
As much as the world outside commands my attention
It is your face I see
Which is pensive as you say, "This is a crazy rain!"
But you are bright faced
When you turn back to me
And I shift my gaze from your reflection
To the real image
You ask about my day
And I tell you something funny
Something at my own expense
You like stories
Where I am a little bit ridiculous
They have the effect I want
Which is your laugh
Or maybe less your laugh
And more the transformation of your face
Once you smile

Lips

Your hallucinogenic scent
Still lingers on my skin
As my fingertip gently circles
Where your lips chose to begin

The Diner's Blessing

Something you see in my eyes
As you speak about the good-looking stranger
Who made a pass at you after one of your gigs
Makes you smile and ask, "Are you jealous?"
"No!" I say too quickly
Though it isn't exactly jealousy I feel
But how we have different ideas about the story we're living together
Because this is the sort of thing you would tell a friend, not a lover
Then I see you make that gesture again with your fingers
That is like a caress
The idea of a caress
But you snatch your hand back quickly
Almost guiltily
When the waitress sets down our desserts
And in the moment before she turns away
I catch a look on her face
That is something more than politeness
A look that is kind
I wonder if she saw your gesture
And read it rightly
Giving it
In a small way
A kind of blessing

Written

Drenched in the scent of our decay
I taste you in my thoughts
With every word I write

Falling in a Diner

You turn your attention
To the plate of dessert sitting before you
Rotating the cheesecake
Until its arrangement pleases you

I love watching you eat
Something you do with a kind of joyful absorption

I watch as you lift
The first bite to your mouth
Then close your eyes with pleasure
Before returning your attention to me
Offering a wink
Something else you know I love

Just What I Didn't Want to Hear

We cross the hot sand, not rushing
Letting it burn the bottoms of our feet
Until we arrive at the shoreline
The water pulls sand from beneath us in small pouches
Above us, gulls, sharply white, scavenge
Bobbing with the sure buoyancy of a kite
I dive into an oncoming wave
The water is icy in a second of suspended time
My heart skips, my lungs gasp, then it is not cold at all
We swim for so long that when we emerge
Our fingers are shriveled, our senses are muted
My ears are plugged, obscuring my hearing
I lay on my towel, tilting my head
First to the left then to the right to drain the water
But I am unsuccessful
You sit beside me, your voice is muffled like underwater thoughts
I have no idea what you are talking about
"I am sorry, can you repeat that?" I ask
Then I feel a warm, ticklish sensation in my ears
The water abates, restoring my clarity
"Sometimes I am afraid to be this happy, Rob, because the happier I am, the
more painful it will be later," you offer sincerely
In an instant I decide
That I liked it better when I couldn't hear

The Diner's Remedy

When I bring it up, you appear uneasy
Shifting in your seat
Playing with the last of the cheesecake
On your plate
Or maybe it's just the wind
For each time it strikes the glass
You lean away from it
"You could just tell them," I say after a minute or so of silence
You look up at me blankly
"About us, I mean. You can tell them about us…"
You make an exasperated
Dismissive sound at my suggestion
I fall silent
As does everyone else in the diner
When a sharper gust of wind
Smacks angrily at the building
It is like being besieged
Before the conversations pick up
And the diner fills again with noise
"You're happy when you're with me, right?" I ask
"You know I am," you say
And it is true
It's something we had already begun to say to one another
That we made each other happy
Because all the hurt we felt vanished
Simply vanished
On the night we finally kissed
It poured a remedy
Over everything we did

The Bully

By midnight
His anxiety has grown
From a drizzle to a typhoon
Accelerating methodically
In violent surges
That chip away at his resolve
Leaving him weak and frayed
It taunts him like the neighborhood bully
Who so wildly underestimated him years before
When he was knocked to the ground more than once
But kept getting back up
Throwing punches at the towering older boy
Who said, "Don't you ever give up?"
And just like back then
He gets up and keeps fighting
Until the bully has had enough

Too Small

Love is a word
That conveys warmth and softness
I love you is everything
When spoken aloud
But I believe
The word *love* needs more letters
More syllables
More resonance to reflect its majesty
Because such a small word
Seems inadequate
To bear so much weight

Breaking Our Silence at the Diner

I watch as you turn back to the window
As though there is something to see out there
In the pitch-black night

I swear I can even see you let go of the fear
When your shoulders drop a little

The wind continues its assault
Its constant charge against the glass
But you aren't flinching from it anymore
Because you're leaning toward the window now
And across the table, closer to me
So close that our foreheads nearly touch

The noise of the diner rises around us
The chatter from the other tables is overlapping
Jumbled and indistinct
Punctuated only by the occasional eruption of laughter
But we stay focused on one another
Until I break our silence and say:
"I want to show you every shade of my heart."

Fiery Storm

As we exit the diner
Immediately we are in it
The rush of wind that steals our breath
Squinting against the grit it carries
Until we are safely inside
In my room
Watching the rain catch morsels of neon
From the streetlamp
Before casting them back up to the sky
The wind makes an accompaniment
A rhythm against which we move
Into our own fiery storm of passion

Orion

When our eyes connect
Desire rushes through my core
As I play with the thought of kissing you
For hours under the evening stars
With a reserved Orion looking on enviously

Contained Desire

As the nearly full moon
Casts its light upon the street
I catch sight of you
Someone so clearly at ease
Walking briskly in my direction
Dressed in white and light blue
With a silver cross glinting on your chest
Which I examine in closer detail
When you and your husband pause to nod hello
But once your gaze grabs mine
I feel myself fall into this strange state of vibrancy
Like a flame sealed off
Submerged in glass
Containing all my desires

Conversation with Myself

Time is a circle surrounded by a growing hurricane
And we are in the eye of it
The experts all say that things
Will get much worse before they get better

I believe them

I don't know how
I am going to keep everyone I love safe
Or if I can
Or what safe even means
But I am going to try

I will
Own my anxiety
Own my voice
Own my love
Own my life
And I'm not giving any of them up
Without a fight

The Watermelon Incident

We carry enormous pieces of watermelon with us
Down to the water's edge
Where we sit at the end of the dock
Dangling our feet in the water
Your boat rocks gently beside us
The waves lap quietly against the sand
Under the August moon that hangs above, half formed
We are surrounded by a chorus of crickets
As we watch a leaf drift lazily on the wind
Before dropping into the water, just beyond our reach
You bite into the moist flesh of the melon
Spitting successions of seeds into the dark
Then you turn and spit the final one at me
It hits my forehead and bounces to the dock
I leer back watching you poke seeds from the melon in your hand
Then without looking up
You draw a finger down my cheek
Leaving a trail of dripping juice
"Really?" I ask
Your response is to take another bite into your watermelon
Purposely allowing its nectar to drip to your chin
Which glimmers in the moonlight
I feel a flush of ardor at the sight
Of you and your chin
Glimmering in the moonlight
I grab the back of your head
And kiss you long and deeply
When I pull back, you are breathless
Offering me a bemused smile
I nudge you and say, "I am not the only one who can be spontaneous, you know!"

Discarded

Watching you
Become more and more insular
Settling into yourself
In small
But significant ways that exclude me
Is as unbearable
As the weeping that burns my cheeks

Seeing this growing distance having emerged
Through my heart's honest confession
Settles me into the understanding
That *we* has shifted to *me*
And that you have already begun rapidly fading
Into the skyline of my dreams

Fear

His fear
Is molten and slow
Climbing inch by inch within him
Like rising water

I Will Remember You Forever, Chuck Dzugan

When my family moved to Westfield in 1972, I was terrified to go to public school because the Catholic school I attended for the first three years of my life was a nightmare, to say the least.

I remember visiting Tamaques School when my mom was finalizing my enrollment. I was amazed by the 1970's open classrooms which were comfy and interactive compared to the dark, cold ones at my old school. The Tamaques classrooms were painted in vibrant colors and had shag carpeting, a sofa, and even a piano. Plus, Tamaques had a gymnasium, a baseball diamond, outdoor basketball courts and a huge yard playground, all the things my old school did not have.

You were one of the first friends I made at Tamaques and the first one to invite me over to your house.

I loved your house and your neighborhood. I was fascinated by all of the houses on North Cottage Place because they were nearly identical, with gigantic basements where we enjoyed sliding across in our socks. You lived on a block with lots of kids from school. That made it easy for me to become friends with Mike, Stu, and Chris and the other boys who lived on or near the block.

In school, you were a good student. Definitely one of the smart kids. You helped me with math and quizzed me relentlessly on the multiplication tables until I had them all memorized.

We both loved books and Mrs. Sullivan's reading class. She was responsible for getting us to read outside of the Encyclopedia Brown books we were obsessed with in those days. She even wanted to move us up to the advanced reading class. So, we made a deal with her to remain in her class. We agreed to read specific books she assigned that were a bit harder than the ones she gave the rest of the class to read.

You excelled in art, and I remember being jealous of your ability to sketch and draw because I couldn't even color inside the lines.

We bonded immediately over our mutual love of music. In Miss Jankowski's fourth grade class, we had a small piano in the classroom, and you taught me how to play "Heart and Soul" on those piano keys. You'd play the low part and I would play the high part. Our classmates used to gather around us when we played it every morning before the final bell.

Goodbye Yellow Brick Road was the first album you ever bought. It was a double album and you purchased it at Music Staff for $5.24. I know the exact total because my memory is like yours. The text like a memory lies on my phone. We both loved Elton John and I remember sitting on the floor of my bedroom with you writing lyrics to the melody of "Lucy in the Sky with Diamonds." I even remember the first line we wrote together. It was a baseball-themed song. I am sure it was inspired by our little league baseball days and it went like this: "Picture yourself on the bench in a ballgame." I wish I was keeping a journal back then because I am sure I would have written down all of our lyrics. However, I am thankful that I remember the first line. When we decided to write a new state song for New Jersey, we wrote lyrics to the tune of the theme from *Hawaii 5-0* and they went like this: "New Jersey is great… beige license plates." I don't remember the other lyrics we wrote, but we did play our new state song for Miss Jankowski and she thought it was great. Later, we performed it together at a school assembly.

Sleepovers were fun at your house; in summer, we would sleep outside in a tent with Chris, Mike, and Stu where we would take turns talking about gross things to see who could make Stu throw up. Poor Stu had a very weak stomach and we totally exploited that!

I was the first one of us to make friends with most of the girls at school, so you and the guys assigned me the task of calling the girls you liked to see if they liked you back. In those days, our crushes changed nearly every week, so I was a busy guy! I always made these calls during a sleepover and then we'd stay up late discussing what each one of the girls had said. In the morning, your mom made the biggest and most delicious pancakes that covered every inch of our plates. When I close my eyes, I can picture us sitting together at your kitchen table eating those pancakes swimming in syrup.

We played a lot of air guitar in your living room as our favorite songs bellowed from the stereo. You loved the famous baseline in Fleetwood Mac's "The Chain" and used to play it from the top of the piano. I never liked KISS but you and Stu loved them. I remember you two rocking out to KISS in your living room with tennis racket guitars pretending to be Paul Stanley and Gene Simmons while I was the audience.

Elton John was your first concert. We went on your twelfth birthday to see Elton play at Madison Square Garden with your mom and Stu. It was 1976 and the concert and sweeping marijuana cloud that hung over the Garden were legendary.

You slept over my house every year on Grammy night and my Mom and Dad let us stay up for the whole show. I remember us both being pissed when Elton lost record of the year to Olivia Newton John in 1975. We threw our pillows at the television in protest. I still think Elton was robbed. I mean, "Don't Let the Sun Go Down on Me" is a way better song than Olivia's breathy "I Honestly Love You," don't you think?

We rode our bikes downtown often and the Westfield Submarine Sandwich was definitely a favorite of ours, but you preferred Duke's over Hershey's. I was the exact opposite, so we used to alternate back and forth between both places whenever we ate subs downtown.

Your favorite football team was the Minnesota Vikings, while mine was the Giants, but you later converted to a Giants fan as an adult.

I was glad when we reconnected in 2010 and it was a pleasure having you be part of my life again after so many years. I was proud to see that you had become an accomplished graphic artist and that playing and writing music was still front and center in your life.

You were a talented musician and composer. I loved the CDs you sent me, and I was in awe of how you could write and play on so many different instruments. Music was a must-do for you, and I understood that as I understood you.

You were complex and somewhat misunderstood, but with you and me it was still simple and uncomplicated. Maybe that is the beauty of a friendship born during our childhood years.

I am still listening to Elton John now as I pen these words. Chuck, I wish your life had led you into a dream that didn't have an ending. I wish we could lie together on your old garage roof and stargaze one more time, so we could speak the language only we understood.

The Bulletproof Vest

The bulletproof vest
He wears to protect his heart
Feels the impact
When shots are fired
But once he is kissed
He forgets about
The searing pain in his chest
And he kisses back
Like the sky is on fire

Bonds of a New Friendship

When you look at me expectantly
Everything goes quiet
Inside, the music blares
I can make out the fuzzy
Happy sounds of chatter underneath it all

Once I begin unloading my angst
You stare at me
With those pesky, enthralling brown eyes
Backed up in their mission
By the most formidable eyelashes

You let me talk
Not saying anything in response
But the way you look at me
With a really kind
Simple look
Tells me
That you are present in the moment
Listening

It is a strange and wonderful thing
To have this from a new friend

The Fragrance of Midnight

I know you from summers at the Jersey Shore
We had always been on friendly terms
But I had my circle
And you had yours
Then in the summer of '96
We ran into one another
Outside the Stone Pony after the Go-Go's show
The night was hot and deep as a kiss
We walked through eclipsed, hushed neighborhoods
Breathing deeply of the succulent sea air
Each of us pointing out places of note along the way
Relating adventures that revealed
Our separate but intersecting histories
Fragrant lilac trees
Of lavender, blue, and violet
Lined the sidewalks
Carpeting Ocean Avenue
As if waiting for a summer bride
I take you to a tree
Bursting with purple blooms
Reaching up, I snap off a stem
Petals rain down like glitter confetti
You give me a high-spirited smile
Blossoms are in your hair
On your nose
On your shoulders
On the bill of your hat
You are beautiful amid the rippling clusters of color
I turn your New York Yankees hat backwards
And kiss you right there
In the fragrance of midnight

Ty's Journal Entry

I was so young when the bullying began that the blame hardly feels like mine. But no matter how minor a part I played, my actions were the most pivotal. Why didn't I ever fight back? Why did I have to be born so different? Why haven't I ever fit in easily with anyone? What is wrong with me? These days I feel like an abandoned sandcastle at high tide washing back out to sea, disappearing little by little. I can't bear to think about living my entire life like this. I don't see anything ever changing. I have no hope. I am a solo act. For as long as I can remember, I have dreamt of meeting someone who can alleviate the loneliness I feel, yet the only people who can are those who know it too. What a sad notion that is. And if you are lucky enough to find one of these people, what then? Father Bill once told me that tears water the soul. I do not believe this because if it were true, my soul would be fertile and verdant. But mine is stunted, gnarled, withered, and cracked. Which is another thing I can't live with. I am so tired of this carefully wrought facade that I project, and it is pointless since the bullies see through it every time and then I realize that I am naked in front of them, so I just run. Run until they catch me because they always catch me. I wish I was more like The Flash so I could outrun anyone, but the tide is coming in again, and this time I will be washed away for good.

A Father's View of Ty's Suicide

Sometimes I walk around
Looking at the fireplace
Or the view from the deck
Or the library room with its shelves of books
Wondering what you had thought and felt
When you'd looked at the same things
Knowing it was for the last time
How could you have been so insensitive
As to go to a place where your loved ones would find you?
And why leave such an enigmatic love poem?
What sort of blackness led to this?
Why didn't I see it, son?
I ponder these questions, feeling detached
Like it hadn't happened to you
But to someone in a movie
I hadn't enjoyed very much

Skin

My skin
Has grown thick
Since you died
All the sorrow
Of losing you
Is sealed in so tightly
That no one else's sadness
Can get through

How We Said Goodbye

I guess some would say it's a bit odd
That the moments when we'd say goodbye
Were among my favorites

There was something about the way
Your eyes shone with their two-toned denim blue color
Right before one of your lingering wet kisses
The way you clung to my hand a little longer
Only letting go when our physical gap
Was too great to stay connected

Your parting smile was different than anyone else's too
Because of how you bit your bottom lip
Revealing a shy vulnerability that very few saw

I do miss our lengthy goodbyes
But I am thankful for my long memory
And my written words
Because these moments
Can never
Disappear

Paint Me

Paint me
Inside your mind
With broad, suggestive strokes

Living Inside the Rush

Inching closer together
We hold on tightly, rooting
Living inside the rush
That makes everything seem possible
With you
Every day means a new beginning
And when we beat the sun in waking up
We feel only the anticipation
And hope
Of its imminent arrival

Dear Derek

I miss how you used to
Break the edges of a New York night
Into tiny pieces
Weaving them
Into rooftop dreams
And mosaic conversations

-R

The Little Prince

I am in the living room, lighting more candles
When I hear your voice at my back door
I run quickly to my bedroom to put on my good shirt
The one that isn't covered in flour and gravy
I had loaned you my new car earlier so I could prepare your birthday
Celebration covertly
But when you find me, it is me who is surprised
Stunned, actually
Your hair has been cut
The curly locks that had framed your face
And flirted with your shoulders are gone
My mouth is agape
You look at me, not understanding
Then you realize, "Oh, I never told you. I get my hair cut
Once a year on my birthday and donate my hair
To the people who make wigs for cancer victims."
I squint and nod my head at your thoughtful generosity
You step over to the two card tables I have set up before the bay window
One is laden with covered pots and pans
The other has two place settings, brass candlesticks, and a large vase filled
with Charleston sea glass
Beside the table is the carrot cake I made along with gifts wrapped (by Alicia
because I can't wrap without lumps and excessive tape) in blue paper with
gold moons and silver stars
I move to where you stand, embracing you and kissing your neck
"I can't believe you did all of this for me and that you knew it was my
birthday," you say, still a bit surprised by everything
"I have my sources," I say playfully with a wink
You slide behind me, arms around my waist, chin on my shoulder
You turn your head and kiss my cheek
"So this is why you gave me your new car?"
"Yup," I say as I bound over and light the candles with a wooden match
Then I pull out a chair and look at you in the heavy dusk
Before I load your plate with baked ziti, meatballs, and antipasto

Lightening flickers in the dusk
And I think how interesting it is that storms have a way of finding us during
every intimate moment we have shared
When we finish dinner, I light the candles of your birthday cake
The flames dance across your shining face
The room is nearly dark now, and we can feel the rain approaching
I hold the cake up, and your eyes flash blue fire in the candlelight
"Thank you, Rob," you say, your breath flickering the flames
Then you close your eyes, make a wish, and blow
Once we each devour a heaping piece of cake, I present you with my first gift
Under the wrapping is a white box
Within the box is a CD I made containing twenty-seven different recorded
versions of "Moon River," the song you play first each time you sit down at
the piano to write
"One for each year," I note
The next box you open houses a vintage hardcover version
Of *The Little Prince*
Your eyes react first, they are enormous and luminous
"Let's read this to one another tonight," you suggest

Later, after the rain, the night grows heavier
We lay together on the porch, reading *The Little Prince*
This ancient house slumbers in the background
Strains of crickets like sleigh bells, come through the screen
As *The Little Prince* reminds us how love allows us to truly see to the heart
and beauty of all things

Painted in Silver

He was different
Tarnished, cloudy, dull and unwanted
Something to scrub away
In the hopes of revealing a prize underneath
He didn't want to be different
But as the years passed
He embraced it

Skies With Unstoppable Sun

There is a light on inside the bookstore
And it gives the shop a soft glow
I have always loved this place
I love the polished floorboards and the deep
Rich wood of the shelves
I love the way the spines of the books look
Aligned neatly, one next to the other

Beyond the front window
Sits the big comfy armchair
Where you always sat
Reading Jack Kerouac on your knee
The books in the windows are new releases on display
From John Grisham, Sebastian Junger, and Mitch Albom
I've read none of them
I look closely at the book at the center of the display
Timequake by Kurt Vonnegut
It has a white cover with gold and black
Lettering with a grey image
Of a watch with Roman numerals
I cannot explain
what it makes me feel, seeing this book
Sadness, maybe, at the pointlessness
Of a book about one of his unfinished works
Or about how time moves from minute to minute
Despite what we have finished
Or that this is a book you'll never get to read
The last time we met here was two weeks ago
You called me over, beckoning me as I walked toward you
Waving until I was close
And then you waved me down at face level
Your breath smelt of peppermint coffee
It came out in white clouds that mingled
With the chilly September air

You wanted us to read
That Kurt Vonnegut book together
You always chose our books
And every week, we would sit atop
Your rooftop garden discussing the chapters

Now, I sit here alone
Outside the Greene Street Bookstore Café
I've bought the Kurt Vonnegut book, Derek
I'll read it for both of us
The city lights float above me
I can feel your breath on my face
How long does it take? I wonder
As I sit on this southbound train
Before I close my eyes and dream
About skies with unstoppable sun and you

Letters

Dear Gregory,

Rob here. I am writing to explain some things about last night. I was wrong about you. You are a nice guy. I liked talking to you in the bathroom. I enjoyed learning about your dog named Spider, the mutt void of a specific breed. I like that you chose him because he was the strangest dog in the shelter, and you thought no one else would take him. I meant what I said last night; I would like to meet him one day. I must confess that I am very selective when it comes to people and animals, but he sounds like he is weird, and I like my people and animals a little weird. Of course, I am weird too, but I gather you know this already. I would like to see your loft and your record collection. If the world ever separated us by music genre, you and I would live in the same city. I think you are going to make a fine human rights lawyer once you graduate from Fordham. I like that you like books. I like you. And the kiss we had was nice, if unexpected. Actually, it was more than nice, it was great. You're a good kisser, Gregory, but there is that guy I told you about. He and I might become serious, so I want to wait to see if that happens. I am really hoping that we can be friends. It will be a long summer in the city if we can't, since we run in the same circles. I hope I get to see you at the Roxy next weekend. Do you skate?

-Rob

Dear Rob,

Thanks for the letter and the explanation. I feel like a bit of an idiot, but your explanation helps. When I drink, I gain courage and if I had been sober, I would not have had the courage to kiss you, but I still would have had the urge to do so. You have my word that I will not try to kiss you again unless you kiss me first. Yes, we can be friends because I like you too. You aren't like the other guys I know in the city. I like that you like conversation and that you are passionate about what you believe. Derek told me a lot about you before we finally met last night. He knows you well. I can skate. I learned to skateboard first before I put on a pair of hockey skates, so roller skates will not be a problem. Well, at least I don't think so! I guess we'll find out next week at the Roxy. Looking forward to it, Rob.

-Gregory

May 8, 1992

The dinner starts quietly
Just as the wind falls
The dining room curtains drop back
I am anxious
But the sudden lack of weight makes me feel giddy
I hold on to the table so I don't float to the ceiling
The others, though, are quite grounded
Avoiding each other's eyes and all conversation
They eat in silence for so long
I begin to wonder how long
They can go without speaking
Until, finally, I pass a plate of mashed potatoes to you
Just as the night air becomes charged with electricity
And the curtains spring in the air
Your dad says, "So Burt tells me you're in love."

Staring Into My Heart

The top of my head prickles
I feel a bit childlike welling up
But I can't continue, not like this
I stand in place for so long
I begin to wonder if you are still
In the room when I finally say, "I'm done."
I am not sure you know what I am talking about
Because between us
There is no context anymore
The silence becomes unbearable
As I stand here naked in my thoughts
Coveting a response
A cry of disbelief
A scream of denial
A sigh of silent resignation
Something, anything
I suddenly become aware
You are not staring at me at all
You are staring into my heart

Panic Attack

I lean heavily against the wall
Sinking to the ground
Clutching my chest
I suck in air through gritted teeth
Trying to stabilize my anxiety

After I manage to take full breaths again
I find my phone
And open the message from you
That I hadn't checked earlier
My eyes fill the moment I read it

It is incredible
The way my fears quell under your words
Like a cloth on a fevered head
I read it over and over again
Just thinking about you
Such simple words
Written from you to me
Are my remedy

The First Time We Made Eye Contact

As Beth and I walk over the dunes and onto Folly Beach
In the hazy midmorning sun, carrying our beach chairs and towels
You are sitting a hundred or so yards away, facing the sea, reading a book

You sit gracefully, your honey-colored hair falls slightly in your eyes
Your tanned skin is offset by the brilliance of your white bathing suit
A pair of gold sunglasses sit atop your nose
You are shining and beautiful like some sort of sand angel

"Isn't that your new neighbor, Robert?" Beth asks
"Yes, I think it is," I reply

As Beth and I set up our chairs and blanket
I glance surreptitiously at you
You are the only other person on this entire stretch of beach
Absorbed in your novel, you are unaware that you are being observed

I make myself wait until I open my bottle of Orangina
Before braving another glance at you
But when you look up from your book and turn directly to me
I stiffen in the incongruent bliss and horror of being caught
Before I turn guiltily away

Honey and Caramel

Nervous energy pours between us
The late September winds stir wildly by
Your eyes dart all around the front porch
Before finally resting on mine

When your hands escape
The confines of your pockets
They rake through your hair
Which looks exactly like a golden mixture
Of honey and caramel
Melted together to perfection

My eyes track the movement
Of your slender fingers through the strands
Wishing my hand could take the place of yours

Fantastically Plotted Best Friend Adventures

The fresh air is my blanket
The sun on my face is a lover's soft-hearted touch
Like a soldier returning from a two-year war
I relish every harmless step I take
On this one-hundred-yard walk
This wooden bench is a familiar old friend
Welcoming me into its curved slats
The waving trees serenely sing to me
In the placid breeze
My journal's pages flap in the wind
With a vibrancy I haven't seen in ages
As my pen kisses its lines, taking me back
To those mild New York City days of January 1997
To the late afternoon walks through SoHo with Derek
We would wander the looping paths passing
The winter-bald patches of lawn on our way
To the commanding fountain in the
Center concrete oval of Washington Square Park
Casting our eyes on the city we loved
Subsumed in its architecture and activity of its pedestrians
We loved how everyone was walking to somewhere
Engaged in their own pursuits
As members of society coursing through their daily circuits
The feeling that we were different from them all
Not in an obvious way
Not to a degree that anyone noticed
Everything returned to us twofold in the end
Leaving us with ideas for more
Fantastically plotted best friend adventures

Once evening set in
Buttery frames of light in the windows
Flickered with the cool panoramic
Glow of televisions

Sometimes we would venture
Beyond the confines of SoHo
Passing a peculiar ground-floor apartment
In Alphabet City
Where a fishbowl window exposed
A warmly lit montage of
Turn-of-the-century Americana
With a multitude of swinging pendulum clocks
A mahogany roll-up desk, and several vintage typewriters
On occasion, Derek and I saw its occupant
An old man with a white *Wizard of Oz* beard
Typing on his shiny black Smith Corona
Looking very much like a man out of time

I miss Alphabet City and its street murals
And buildings of a similar shade of graphite
I miss seeing the Empire State Building's white lights
Shining despite a shawl of rainy fog
I miss seeing the pavement shimmer
With the puddled reflection of streetlamps
I miss the damp wind making the oak trees
Creak under a pewter sky
I miss New York, and I miss Derek
There was something about these 1997 moments
They were brighter, more exceptional, and exquisite
I felt compelled to write them down and memorize them
To capture their essential, truthful quality
So, years later, my retrospection
Would not be altered in subtle ways

I put down my pen, close my journal
And stand on my battered feet
I never saw this coming
The deep sense of loss I feel as I walk
The one hundred yards back home
I tell myself it is okay to feel sad
Because it is a loss

But I still have both my feet and
I still live close enough to the city
To go in and enjoy its majesty
Derek is no longer of this world
 But I have Kai, and he is just as remarkable
My ability to walk is limited
And my pace is much slower 24 years later
But I still hear all three heartbeats of the city
Beckoning me to return
I cannot wait to write down and memorize
More New York moments with Kai
As we bathe in the light
We create living inside
The heartbeats of the city

The America I Believe In

There is beauty everywhere
Hidden in everything
Even in today's hate-filled climate
Like the light through the clouds
The shadows in the mountains
The flashing colors of the ocean
The smiles of people who might not be perfect
Who have every reason to be miserable
But still find small ways to be kind to each other

This is the America that I believe in

Dear Derek (3/6/2021)

I have read that people have loads of sex to get over the grief, but I never did that. Ricardo and I broke up. I pushed him and our sex life away after I lost you. I haven't kissed anyone since him. I don't want to kiss anyone. I don't want to see anyone kiss anyone. I definitely don't want to see Ricardo kiss his new cop boyfriend.

I am tired of explaining, Derek. I am tired of people questioning my grief. I have grown used to others not understanding my grief. They think I shouldn't be grieving so long since you weren't my blood or my lover. I have grown used to being alone and doing my own thing. I have grown used to skipping out of work to sleep more. I need to stop that. I have grown used to crying in my room where no one can see.

I went to the supermarket today and I found myself in the candy aisle, staring at the M&M's. I missed how you and I would stand in the candy aisle, deliberating between the peanut and the peanut butter M&M's. Today, I put both bags in my cart.

I am eating too much and not moving enough, Derek. I have turned into a zombie who hides in his room eating bags of M&M's until he falls asleep. At night, when I wake up, I drive to the beach and walk the shore alone because I feel you there. Sometimes, I lie in the back yard with the sun in my face and the warm grass at my back, with my eyes closed so I can see you. So I can see us.

I don't want to hide, and I don't want to be miserable anymore, Derek. I need to begin living again; not just for me, but for you too.

-R

The Elusive Shore

There isn't a specific image
That comes to mind when I think of you
But that Elton John song
"Something About the Way You Look Tonight"
Comes to me
The words run through my head in a loop
Like the black numbers on a gas pump
The refrain chases me
Until I can retreat
And escape into the music of a different song
One with countless layers of rhythms
Melodies
And lyrics
With the hope that one of them will catch
Resulting in my fleeting freedom
But every time, like the insistence of an undertow
The melody returns
Mournful
Pleading
Provoking

All of this makes me wonder how others shake their grief
Or if, no matter how heavily they weigh it
How often they send it plummeting to the depths
Certain it is gone for good
They're astonished to find it bobbing joyfully
Cynically, spitefully
Each time they turn for shore

You Forgot About Me Once, You'll Forget About Me Again

Everyone has been telling me
That I should patch things up with you
But patching up is not a possibility
Because I can't patch up
You forgetting about me
For the rest of my life I'll wonder
If you'll forget about me again

More than Anything, I Want You to Write Me a Song

The summer night is humid
Lightning flashes on the steamy horizon
The clouds that block the moon are puffy with rain
The wind cuts sideways through the convertible
I look at the water watching the mirrored lightning
Pretending I am looking at the storm upside down
From the inside of a polished wine glass
You turn the car away from the shore
And we become enclosed on both sides by trees
I can hear the wind rushing in the leaves

Before the storm rolled in
We had gone hunting for sea glass
When the tide was out
Squatting over tide pools
With your nephew's sand bucket
We had walked far
Following the shoreline
Passing the summer rentals, rock formations
And the dilapidated Holiday Inn
Our hunt had only yielded two pieces
Of green sea glass
But we did find a sand dollar

Once we arrive back at your house
We sit next to each other quietly on the porch
A mist of mosquitos hangs over the yard
Fragrant lightning bugs flare back and forth
From beside the front steps
When I close my eyes softly
My mind drifts to when I watched you write a song
I stood inside, viewing you through the screen
I didn't observe what you were writing, I observed you
The way your mouth drew down to the left

When you couldn't get something right
But when everything did come together just right
You strummed your Fender guitar mercilessly
Tilting your head back, moving it side to side
I watched you lean into the song
As your long black hair fell onto alternating shoulders

I want more than anything for you to write me a song
To be important enough to have the memory of my presence honored
I hear the screen door slam, and it snaps me back into the present tense
Looking up, I notice that the evening has lost its luster
Perhaps I have lost mine too because you have gone inside without me
Suddenly, it occurs to me that I need you more than you need me
And I don't know if you know that yet

Reflection Fire

It was unexpected and effortless
Like something from a previous life
Familiar yet new
In a place filled with art in the margins
The fiery reflection in your eyes
Brings oranges and reds to the darkness of the room
As we discuss our artistic endeavors
Time is fleeting because I recognize what is happening
I am caught in the eye of an artistic hurricane with you
That sounds like a melody that builds on its way to the bridge
But we don't reach the bridge
Because eternity breeds better harmonies

Deeper Than Bone

The feelings for you that I possess
Shatter in silence
Breaking deeper than bone

Dread and Absurdity

I frown back at my own
Reflection in the mirror
Filled with dread
I look sad
More than that
I look confused with myself
With how I am capable
Of feeling lost before
I have lost anything yet
I felt this way last year
Before things ended abruptly with my job
I step away from the mirror and breathe
Inhaling in and out, in and out
Suddenly, the impending day
Stops feeling so aggressive
Because I have begun to accept
The absurdity of my situation

The Lexus

On the way to your beach house
All I can think about is you
I play the CD you made me
Singing along to all your songs
As they play through

Once I arrive
I am surprised to see the Lexus
His Lexus
In the driveway

"What is he doing here?"
A flicker of dread passes through me
Like a bolt of lightning

Your mom's scarlet and
Lemon-colored geraniums
Greet me when I reach the porch
I knock on the screen door
But there is no answer
The front door is ajar
So I decide to enter
Once inside I hear muffled voices
Coming from upstairs
I snap the rubber band
I wear on my wrist
Repeatedly
To ward off my anxiety
As I climb the stairs

My hand
Is on the hallway light switch
When I pause

Hearing a sound from your bedroom
Someone is crying
It sounds like you
I gingerly walk the remaining steps
To your closed door
Ignoring the slight sense of shame
That overcomes me for eavesdropping
"Please reconsider me."
Are the words I hear him say
I jump away from the door
My nerves are so surged with electricity
That my skin itches
I stumble around the corner
Standing with my back up against the wall
Trying to subdue my breathing
And the booming of my heart

The muffled conversation continues
As I soundlessly descend the stairs

Back in my car
I turn the music up loud
Attempting to dispel
The screaming thoughts in my head
When the song "I Can't Wait" comes on
The irony is not lost on me
I lean into Stevie's fiery vocal
As she demands her lover to make up his mind

The sun is setting
When I pull up to the restaurant
I sit facing the water
I feel the pounding of the surf
It is loud and sounds like a robust engine
Shifting the world to another place

It is still hard to breathe

The lack of air in my lungs
Messes with my equilibrium

I stare out the window for a long time
Considering you, considering us
Or perhaps what is left of us
Eventually I take out my journal and write
Spilling fragmented thoughts on its pages
Until the pen is abruptly
Snatched out of my hand
It's you
I look up and examine your eyes
They look as relieved as I feel
Affable, polite, and caring
Once you take hold of my hand
Oxygen pours back into my lungs

Denial

It is not the first time
I've heard you're not right for me
Kai thinks you're boring
That you don't have any style
Nick thinks you are too young for me
Ed doesn't like the way you turn up
At my house when you're lonely
Only to disappear when you're not
But it isn't like that
It is more like you cannot stay
Away from me any more than I
Can stay away from you
I always take you back
I will always take you back
I might tell myself I won't
But then you show up and it feels
Like something out of my control
You're my destiny
You're not anyone else's destiny

I stumble through the crowd
Trying all the while to figure out
What to say to you when I arrive
The words to get you back exist
I just have to work out the order of them
But I've got nothing
I stand in front of you and him
Staring and swaying
Then I fixate on your hands,
Which are entwined together
"This is so disturbing," I say
Surprised I have said this out loud
You raise an eyebrow at me without
Dropping your hand from his

The two of you are still entwined together in front of me
A week ago, you were entwined with me
Standing there, I think about a lot of things
I think how you probably hate that I am so old school
That I am so emotionally intense
That I don't have an unlimited bank account
That I don't have a perfect body
I never thought any of this mattered, but maybe it does
Maybe this is why you keep going away and coming back
You come back because you can't stop loving me
You leave because I don't have everything you want
I need to become everything you want
"I want you to come home with me," I say defiantly
Maybe it's the light but I don't think it is
You look unsure
One second of uncertainty tells me
Everything I need to know
I can have you back if you change
Then, the guy you're with pushes me slightly
But it is just enough to make me fall
Backward into a crowd that instinctively
Clears a space for me
I look up from my position on the floor
You look down on me sadly
In those eyes, I read something
I read that you want me to change
"If you change," your eyes scream
"I'll come running back."

The Library of You

The entire neighborhood is asleep
Except for me
The candle burning on the table
The porch light above
I sit on the floor
Sifting through the songbook you left here
Treating it like the library of you
I have been going for two hours now
Entering your thoughts
Imagining what you were thinking
As you wrote these lyrics and notes
I flip through your pages
Looking for the song you wrote
About disturbing the status quo
You got the idea for the song
From your favorite poem of mine in *tide pool*
Where I mention my desire
To "smash the globe that holds the status quo"
You sang it to me here only three weeks ago
But it feels more like a couple of light years ago now
We were lying on the floor of the porch
And as you sang, it felt like a love song
Gazing at the candle burning next to me
I hear your baritone voice singing.
"We have lingered in the chambers
of expectation too long; do you dare
disturb the status quo with me?"
I remember as you sang
I stared at the mark on the ceiling
The one the Christmas garland left
It looked like a tear shaped ray of sunlight
Lying there next to you
With your voice so close to my ear
I wanted to disturb something

I wanted to disturb us
Shake us out of seeing
One another as rebound lovers
I loved the song for the lines
About disturbing the status quo
That said something to me about
The life I had been living
After the song you put your guitar
Back in the case and closed your songbook
Before shifting your position sideways
And using my thighs as a pillow
I watched as you closed your eyes
Snoring softly after a while
I took the songbook from your sleeping
Fingers and read the lyrics aloud in a whisper
Tonight, I study the same songbook
Seeing the lyrics and lines you underlined
I hear the song in your voice
Having this strange thought as I read
How can this songbook hold the memory
Of that night so clearly?
My memories are trapped in the words of this song
Everyone who hears you sing it
Will have my memories now
And not even know it
Maybe they will love
The same words that I do

Best Friend Haiku

Stones of promises
Built across assurances
A perfect friendship

New York Night

I meet Derek at the Canal Street subway station
He is dressed in Armani
Looking every bit like the Armani model he is
Holding two fat pretzels, one for each of us
And we hop the C-train to the Upper West Side
To some actor's West Side loft
Once there, Derek presses the button and we are buzzed in
I can hear the music a soon as we're through the lobby door
Depeche Mode is singing "It's No Good"
Which I am already sick of
Because it has been playing everywhere in the city for months
Derek makes the rounds, saying hello
To other models and actors he recognizes
I don't know anyone here and I hate feeling like I don't belong
So I hang back and grab a beer from the cooler
In the eerie light, I start looking through the bookcases
You can tell a lot about people by what they read
While I am not particularly intrigued in the private interests of this actor
It at least makes me look like I am doing something
"Have you read that one?"
I turn to see a guy wearing a Red Sox cap backwards
Pointing to the spine of a book that reads *Brideshead Revisited*
"Not yet," but I watched the BBC miniseries
"Take it and read it, my brother won't mind."
The guy has olive skin and a cute, timeless look
With a slight scent of cinnamon
From the cinnamon-flavored Big Red gum he is chewing
Brown eyes and dark curly hair that is short
Combed away from his face
No fancy clothes, no effort
He is dressed casually in a Santana concert t shirt and jeans
He is visiting from UMass for the weekend
And loves baseball as much as I do
But thankfully we avoid the Yankees/Red Sox debate

"This party isn't really my thing either," he says, smiling easily
I find myself smiling back, slightly overwhelmed
"Parties aren't my thing," I confess
"I came here with my best friend, Derek, he is friends with your brother."
The music changes and catches my attention
My confusion must be obvious
Because he looks at me for a minute
Before offering Daft Punk's "Around the World"
"I have no idea what it is about
But it is pretty cool, very New York."
In his innocence, he thinks this is more New York than New York itself
I sometimes wonder about the New York that only exists
In the mind of a visitor
I find this interesting
And I share with him my view of New York
Which is so much more than the clubs, the music, and the nightlife
Because when you walk around the city
There is a story waiting to be told around every corner
This is the real essence of New York
We talk about our cities and each one of us gains a new perspective
It is a thoughtful and informative conversation
And I come away knowing so much more about Boston
And how its essence is about the families that go back generations
And not just a city filled with ardent sports fans
Beer drinkers, and seafood restaurants
Although he has a laid-back appearance
He is intense and passionate when he speaks and that draws me in
"I have the new Talking Heads album on cassette," he says
Gesturing down the hallway at a closed door
He looks at me expectantly and I feel a flash of attraction and curiosity
I usually assume that any guy who talks to me about books and music
Is hitting on me, but something about this guy is different
He is unassuming, or maybe I'm different
Maybe it doesn't even matter, maybe it is simply time for me to stop waiting
For everyone else to tell me what to do or what not to do
Maybe it is time just to be myself
Before I can chicken out I channel Derek's confidence

And say, "Lead the way!"
Following him to the guest room
The room looks like a holding tank for 1975
With its shag carpet, lava lamps, and beaded curtain
Derek wasn't lying about his actor friend being a little obsessed
With the 1970s and Studio 54, because this room is proof of that
I watch as he moves a brown furry pillow to uncover
A yellow Sony Walkman
He takes the cassette out and puts it in a blue boombox on the dresser
The only thing here that belongs to this decade
The music begins and as we listen
He tells me he is leaving in the morning on a train back to Amherst
Two songs in, David Byrne sings about wanting to be home
And already being there
When we hear a knock on the door; it's Derek
He opens the door and sees me
Suspended in some sort of fleeting happiness
The sincerity of my eyes tells him everything
He knows that I am ready to leave
The Red Sox guy turns his face illuminated by the purple of the lava lamp
I feel the tension leave my body in one gush
As I nod my head at him and say, "It was nice meeting you."
He takes a step toward me, his face serious
"I am sorry you have to go," he says
While reaching out his hand
Putting it on my arm
His voice is soft
He still smells of cinnamon, his fingers calloused
And the roughness of them against my skin
Makes me flush as my head fills with warnings
Derek sees what is happening here
He knows that I am lonely
But he also knows that I am looking for permanence
Not something fleeting
On our way out, he looks over at me for confirmation of this
I bow my head to him and whisper
"It is not like I am ever going to see this guy again."

The Second Time We Made Eye Contact

The next day is a hot, humid, 98 degrees. It is too hot for me and Beth to go to the beach again, so I head to, The Sea of Books, instead, my favorite bookstore on the island.

Inside, the store is cool, and I quickly grab the new Pat Conroy book, *Beach Music,* from just inside the door, pausing a bit so my eyes can adjust. The bookstore is silent except for the occasional whispering of pages, but then my pupils widen when I see you materialize from the Stephen King section. What strikes me most is that you are even more attractive up close. Your cheekbones are weightless, your lips soft like summer rain. Your golden hair falls haphazardly onto your smooth, tanned skin. You have soulful, sad eyes, rimmed in gold, which are a lustrous pale blue. I cannot help but gawk as dust motes from the sun beaming through the store window stream between us like little comets. Then you look at me. I gasp lightly, not at being caught, but at the magnificent way you look me in the eye, leaving me quietly wondering if I will ever be the same.

The Beginning of Us

The first time you show yourself to me
We are walking together
Along this quiet stretch of Folly Beach
The one that gets more and more silent
The closer you get to the river
And when a fast-moving summer storm erupts
Drenching us in a matter of seconds
It is the first time I feel the joy of heavy rain

Dancing Infernos

Cinnamon mingles with vanilla
Lips brush lips
Infernos dance down their spines

The Elevator

Once the elevator doors shut
The energy changes
Everything about this enclosed space tingles
The rush of my pulse is so loud
I am sure you can hear it pounding
When I turn to look at you
I find you looking back
You are wearing a grey hoodie
And washed-out jeans
The absence of color
Makes your eyes a crazy shade of blue
A picture of Bora Bora
But without any green
Pure and bottomless
Then you smile back
And I realize that we both
Have instinctively leaned in
Toward the other
As if some outside force
Is pulling us in against our will
But just as this is happening
The elevator chimes and the doors open
Others enter and invade our tiny space
When I look over again
You are missing

The Attack

He approaches as we exit the restaurant
Rage radiates from his face so strongly
That I can look at nothing but him
I recognize him from the hotel
I fired him yesterday
He moves quickly
Like a tornado racing across an open plain
For a moment, I fear for our lives
He steps forward, raising an arm
My mouth explodes as I fall onto the pavement
Darkness begins seeping into my eyes
Blood courses my mouth
I crawl to my knees
Spitting out a dense dollop of blood
The blackness recedes
And I see you nose to nose with him
The words you speak are measured and concise
Each one carrying the weight of a threat
"Get away from him, now!"
I watch your fists land on his face
In a succession of blows
Their force knocks him out cold
Someone inside calls the police
You lean over me
Eyeing my blood-stained face
I feel your warm hands on each side of me
Before you gently take my hand and help me up
My mouth is throbbing
Your breathing is loud and hot in my ear
I look to you
Your eyes are the opaque blue of an iceberg
I swallow my fear so thoroughly
Hoping to extinguish any trace of my humiliation
When you move closer, you pull me in

Placing my head softly against your chest
Immediately
I am hit by your shirt
It smells of Folly Beach
And I nearly smile
You hand me back my watch
The one with the worn-out band
It must have fallen off when I was hit
You put my watch back on my wrist
Because my free hand is holding the ice pack the EMT gave me
When our eyes meet again
Mine are wet, dark, and apologizing
They speak to you soundlessly

My attacker is conscious now
Facing us before he is led into the back of the patrol car
My fingers pulse like vicious hearts
I grapple to find words to articulate my contempt for him
He spits savagely
With malicious prejudice
In my direction
But his aim is not good, and it lands to my right
Amongst a smoker's discarded cigarette butt
I see you lock eyes with him
Throwing an intimidating glare his way
It works because he looks down and away
You let loose a heavy breath and say,
"Let's go home."
I can see your heartbeat through your chest
My blood is on the front of your shirt
I give you a light kiss on the lips
Passing along the taint of fresh blood
You kiss me back and laugh into my mouth saying,
"Now that is a bloody kiss!"

New York, New York

I only have a moment to decide
If I want to see you one last time
Before I have a chance to voice my answer
I find myself following a man
In a white coat to the elevator
I watch the numbers descend
Until the elevator doors open
The man in the white coat leads the way
He holds the door and I enter
I hesitate, not sure I can do this
I take a deep breath
And quietly approach you
Your body is unmoving
I know you are dead
It feels real now
Your skin has lost its pinkness
Replaced by a tinge of blue-grey
With darker rings around your lips and eyes
Your eyes are closed
I wish I could see them one more time
Above us I hear voices and footsteps
I lean over your body
I can't cry
Not yet
Not here
I know it is you
But I cannot reconcile *this you* now
I lean in so I can look directly into your face
My breath is in such close proximity
That it rebounds off your corpse
From somewhere in the past
I hear Frank Sinatra singing "New York, New York"
Muted as if we are standing
Outside Yankee Stadium after the last out

It gets louder as I rock back and forth on my feet
The song becomes a clamor
I take your right hand
And bring it to my face
I hear the door creak open behind me
The song roars thunderously
Until I feel dizzy and terrified
There is not enough air
The threat of shame
At being caught overwhelms me
The song's melody becomes dissonance
Your hand drops from my face
And warmth
Abandons my world

The First Time You Opened Up to Me

You reach out and put your hand on mine, rubbing your thumb gently over my knuckles. You look up at me and say, "My future has seemed so empty and irrelevant since Roy died. All the things I wanted from my life, I kind of stopped wanting. And nothing else has stepped up to fill in the space. But lately…" Your voice trails off and your eyes drop, out of shyness or embarrassment or both, and your thumb stops moving over the top of my hand for a moment. Then you pick up my hand from the table and turn it over, cupping it between yours. I watch this, mesmerized for a minute, before lifting my eyes back to yours and finding that you are staring right at me. A small smile is on your face.

"Things have felt different since I met you, Robert," you say. My heart leaps and I smile back at you. Unfortunately, our waitress chooses this moment to interrupt, and you let go of my hand.

We eat without revisiting this topic, choosing instead to dive into our patty melts and disco fries. Later, when we leave the diner and I drive you back to your apartment, I can still feel the imprint of your touch against my skin. I keep running your words over and over in my mind, wishing I could hear them again and again for the first time.

The First Time You Opened Up to Me II

We arrive at your apartment; you reach for the door handle, but then, instead of getting out of the car, you slide across the seat to me and run a hand around my waist, pulling me in. I react without thinking, reaching up with my right hand to grab the back of your head and pull you toward me, so our foreheads are touching.

Since I met you, I have been telling myself that something like this could not happen, but now that it has, it feels like everything since then has been leading up to this.

"Let's pick up this conversation next time," you say, turning and jumping out of my car. I watch as you run down the gravel driveway and through your front door, without looking back.

As I drive away, my face is still flushed and warm, so I open the windows to let in some air, but the warm breeze does little to cool the memory of your hand around my waist.

Midnight Kiss in Costa Rica

On our last day in Costa Rica, it pours. Relentless boredom sets in
I sit with everyone else in the living room of this beach bungalow
Not reading the Stephen King book on my lap
You stand at the sliding glass door, watching the rain pelt your reflection
Someone suggests we go to the pool hall in town
You give an enthusiastic thumbs up
And when you do, I make eye contact
Attempting to assemble the pieces of the puzzle
Left from last night on the beach, when you, an alleged straight guy
Leaned in and surprised me with a hot midnight kiss
We don't have enough umbrellas for everyone
So you and I share one, but we are still soaked when we reach the pool hall
We burst through the front door in a dissonance of voice
Our shoes squish on the floor on the way in
You and I settle into two seats at the bar, water from your dark curly hair
Trickles down your neck onto your shirt, a glimmer of white in the dim light
All the swirling emotions I've had since our midnight kiss come raging forth
You look at me with those eyes, those marvelous eyes
So bright like they are lit from within
I feel myself detach my gaze, intimidated by their color
Immersed in warm, comfortable light. But I can't lose myself yet
You are looking at me, but I don't know what to say
I look down at your white shirt and white linen shorts
Your hands are large and your fingers long; you're flawless
I am so mesmerized I don't notice you reaching out
You take my hand into your own and for an instant, all I can think about
Is how easily your hand envelopes mine
How your cool, dry, fingers whisper along the underside of my wrist
My heart rejoices at the sensation of your touch until you say,
"That kiss last night, it was just an impulse. Something I wanted to try."
I hear what you say, but I don't believe you because your eyes say something
Much different. I can't pull myself away from your gaze
You smile a warm, genuine smile back
Your teeth are as white as the glare of a freshly painted picket fence
I feel a flutter in my chest—I want to kiss you again
So I lean in and do just that, in front of everyone
And much to my surprise, you kiss me back

Taming the Turbulence

The sudden squall catches us by surprise
I follow you out to the screened in front porch
The air is damp and chilly
The sky is shadowy and ominous
We can hear the heavy pelting of rain above
I rub your arms and ask if you're cold
Slipping off my T-shirt, I give it to you
Before you have a chance to respond
We sit, waiting out the storm
My arms around you
Hands inside our shirts
Fingers against your abdomen
Once the storm ends
We step out into the bright and overcast day
Our skin is riddled with gooseflesh
Your enormous eyes
Look just like the turbulent blue-black
Of the violent sea
The rain is over
But the air is still heavy
Up above, gutters run noisily
Branches litter the lawn
I spend the remainder of the day
Sitting on the porch stairs
Watching you strum your guitar
There is something about your eyes
Whenever you play
They appear enormous
More luminous and dazzling
So much so I fear drowning in their depths
Your voice is soothing as you hum along
To your newly written melody
It is just what I need to hear
After such turbulence

Tripping My Usual Sense of Balance

The gigantic house
Across from our bungalow intrigues us
It appears uninhabited, or at least it is
For the time we have been here
It has especially large windows that face the sea
They are so big that it makes us wonder
How small someone on the inside would look
To us, these windows seem cold
Like hardwood floors in winter
From the beach, they look like eyes
Reflecting the sky: blue, pink, and white
As we lie together, on the floor of the porch
We wonder in tandem what the house might be thinking
To cause its eyes to turn murky blue or metallic grey
You wake us from this thought
By nudging me in the arm and asking.
"Want to get some ice cream?"
"Yes," I say with a smile
Because I am already imagining the taste
Of fresh Costa Rican mango ice cream

The inside of the ice cream parlor
Is bright and shiny
With yellows, oranges, and reds
When I hear you order for me
I feel bliss radiate from within
Shivering with goosebumps on my flesh
I give you a nervous smile and say,
"I suppose someone walked on my final resting place."
"What does that mean?" You ask inquiringly
"It means someone in the future
Walked over your final resting place
So it causes you to shiver in the present
The Irish witches on my mom's side of the family informed me of this once

And I have always believed."
"You're interesting, Rob
First your Scrabble fetish and now this," you say with a squint
I watch as you order two Cokes
And grab us napkins on the way to the table
It is surprising, this content feeling I have
Of being taken care of this way
You have tripped my usual sense of balance
Here in Costa Rica
And I absolutely love that

A Hint on Our Skins

Your smile
Is warm and kind
You have a swath of milk
On your upper lip
Which is just about the sexiest thing
I have ever seen
Your eyes are soft and powder blue
Like my mother's
I like you immediately
Which feels a bit odd
Since I usually don't react
So profoundly to strangers
But I don't feel
Like you are a stranger at all

When I met you earlier
And we shook hands
We both held on a for a few extra seconds
In that instant I thought
Maybe I've discovered
What I've been looking for
Without even realizing
I've been looking for something
You feel like déjà vu
Because my world suddenly makes sense
It is like waking up to a dream
Instead of reality
With our love
Just a hint on our skins

The World We Have Created

The person I was before is gone
You have changed me
It is unsettling to so be so new
As I towel off in the shower
The sight of my naked torso
In the mirror snags me
I look different
Though I cannot say why
I lean over and probe my pupils
Like I am looking through a peephole
To see what has changed
I peer until I realize
I am staring back at myself
Am I really as handsome as you say?

When I go downstairs
In my burgundy shirt and shorts
I am shaky
My bravado from the afternoon has fled
I want to cry
Not because I am afraid or insecure
Or regret what we did in bed
The emotions are just too much
I need an outlet
I stand at the sliding glass door
Looking out at the sea
Attempting to control my feelings
I hate being the emotional one
I wish I were more like Justin
Who sails through life
Never doubting himself, never wavering
Tears slip out as I stand there
Comporting myself with as much dignity as possible
I jump when I feel your hand on my back

I swipe angrily at the tears
Before turning around to face you
"You okay, Rob?" you ask, with concern in your voice
"I'm fine," I manage
You follow me out to the porch
Where we are greeted by the roar of the surf
The sun is shooting reds, oranges, and greens across the water
The tenderness of lilacs mingles with the savory sea air
My shirt billows around my body
The smooth, cool wind dries my tears
I lean on the railing, inhaling deeply
So nervous my teeth are chattering
When I turn my head, I am once again
Greeted by your simple, understated beauty
I look at you, judging the sincerity of your smile
While listening with subdued reverence as you say,
"Let's just live in the moment for the rest of this trip, Rob."
In the remaining sunlight your tan skin glows translucently
With a halo of fiery color about your head.
"Would you…" I say with a smile that comes out goofy
"Would you like to play Scrabble?"
"Sure," you say with a nod
And just like that, a cool calm rushes back into this world
The world you and I have created here in Costa Rica

Dear Derek (3/8/2021)

I hope you don't mind that I summoned you into my dream earlier. I needed to see you and New York together again. You were on my mind every second today, but how can I not think about you on a day I am lost and struggling with everything? You never remembered your dreams, Derek, so here is a recap: In the dream, we went to a quiet corner of the city where nobody knew us and we ate gyros overflowing with lettuce, tomato, onion, and hummus and dangled our legs over the ledge above the Hudson River. We gazed across at the New Jersey side, breathing in tandem just as we did on our last New Year's Day together in 1997. Lingering with you was always my favorite thing. It felt good to be like this again with you, Derek. You understood everything without me saying a word. The last thing said before I woke up was, "Don't worry if you're unable to walk, Rob, I will carry you home in every storm."

This probably sounds absurd but sometimes I have difficulty believing you are dead because in my dreams and in my memories, you are still alive. I can't make my brain absorb the realization that I will never see you again. I hate forgetting, only to remember. I know you see the sadness I hide from others. I write to keep you alive. I write to keep you from dying again. The rational part of me knows that my words don't really bring you back to life. Does any of this make sense? Sometimes I think to myself, what is the point of these words if I can't say them directly to you? If I can't look you in the eye and watch you digest every syllable? Then I remind myself that these words I write to send out to my readers keep us both alive.

-R

What I Need Most Today

Your hair is tousled
There is something so sexy
About its messiness
That I fight the urge to touch it
Since it is your eyes I am looking for today
To settle my uneasiness
Because those dark brown eyes
Can calm my spiked heartbeat
At a glance

Shifting World

I rub my eyes
Feeling like the world
Has shifted on its axis
You let out an extended sigh
And lean your head back
Onto the rail of the stairs
Your eyes toward the half moon

I lean my shoulder into yours
You smile faintly
Before the reality of what you said
About leaving
Slaps me in the face

Next to You

We sit and watch the sunset
In perfectly contented silence

Off in the distance
The city lights provide
Pillars of electric color

We don't leave from our perch
Until the stars are out
And we have seen the world
Go to sleep
Together

Whispered Comforts

It is a relief
To finally tell you
Everything
To let it all out
Losing Derek
How I failed with Ricardo
How everything is ruined now
It is a relief to cry
And hear you say that my response is correct
I feel exhausted after telling you
Everything
I leave out my trip to the morgue
Because I can't ever talk about that
With anyone
Not even you

I feel almost as tired as I did
In the days after I took Derek to the hospital
For the last time
We sit on the bench
The one at the head of the quad at Princeton
You and I came here for a literary event
Hosted by a former professor of yours
But we haven't moved from this bench
And I am sure we have missed the lecture by now

I feel like running
Sometimes I wish I could swim all day long
Drowning out every sound of the world
And sometimes I just want to sit
 In the same place forever
Because I don't have the energy
For another day without Derek in it
I can see Derek at the counter of the bookstore

Taking mints from the free bowl
Rolling them up and down the counter
While he speaks to Keith
Keith loved Derek
He loved telling him
Strange facts about writers
When Keith joined us for Sunday night pizzas

After a while, it begins to rain softly
There are sparks in the humid sky
"We need to go," you say
You're not a fan of thunderstorms
"Maybe I'll just sit here," I offer
"It'll stop raining soon."
"No," you insist
While reaching down a hand
Pulling me up
It begins to pour
You start running and it feels good
To run with you
To be moving and laughing again
I count the seconds between the lightning and thunder
Once we get to the car, you stop and fumble
With the keys before unlocking the doors
I don't want to go home. I want to stay here
In your car and talk until we find the silence
The peaceful silence, not the disturbing silence
That I have come to know so well

I say this to you, and you look relieved
That there is something practical you can do
And we do find the peaceful quiet after a while
I look out at the rain that is falling beyond the window
Lit up by streetlights so every separate line of water is visible
Thinking about the dream I had the other night
Where Derek told me he could see the world from up above
You stretch out your arm so I can use it as a pillow

"What else can I do to help?" you ask in a whisper
"Distract me."
"I can do that," you say
With one of your trademark smirks
"I'm very distracting, you know."

Buoyancy of Anticipation

"The beauty of low tide is fleeting, so we should revel in it," I say
Not sure if I am talking about you or the blue green water
Landing softly on the sandbars
I feel like I am teetering on the edge of a precipice
As if I could lose my balance at any time
I look over and see you push
Your hair behind your ear
It is a sexy move, perhaps a deliberate one
It makes me feel a little out of control
So I look away quickly and out to the sea
Inhaling deeply the salt air
Burying my feet deeper in the sand
"Most people don't bother getting to know me," you say
Releasing your breath
It's not quite a sigh and when I turn back
I look at you silently
For a minute before saying, "I'm different."
You touch my arm, causing the hair on it to stand up
The place where your flesh meets my own
Is so alive it is painful
My nerves are screaming at attention
I want to pull my arm away because it is too much
Then your fingers are gone and I can breathe again
We look at each other openly for many seconds
Savoring this new, warm, welcoming
Buoyancy of anticipation
We have just found

Sliver of Time

The unseasonably warm night air lacquers our skin
When the chorus of "Stop Draggin' My Heart Around" begins
Our dancing grows crazier
Like spinning tops wobbling out of control
Your dark eyes look aqueous when the light strikes them
A coy smile of flirtatious teasing rings in
An intimate possibility on this New Year's Eve night
We sway into one another like we are in the April of our lives
As Stevie Nicks and Keith Urban continue
Singing on the television
I keep turning my eyes up to yours squinting at mine
They shoot an electric charge through me
We smile tightly, leaning into the bliss
Leaving behind our clamped shut hearts
Inside this sliver of time, we live a lifetime
Because the high on this homemade dance floor
Has yet to wear off

Only in New York

You down your espresso
Setting it on the counter
Wiping a few drops
With your monogrammed handkerchief
The alarm on your watch chimes
It is time to go
The 6-train arrives at the Canal Street station
As we pump our tokens into the turnstiles
We race to the doors
You lead the way
Invigorated by the task of making the train
It is hard to remember
The last time I ran anywhere like this
I leap across the threshold
Smacking my head on the frame
Of the subway car
It feels like someone just clocked me
On the head with an iron skillet
You hear the collision and turn to see me wincing
"You good?" you ask while gently lifting my chin
And rubbing my head
"How very *French Connection* of you, Rob," you say
Trying to lighten the mood
I nod and grin at your iconic
New York film reference
A man I have seen periodically
On the subway enters the car
He wears a battered NY Yankees hat
And large sunglasses that cover most of his face
Under his arm is a violin
We both watch as he sets up his tip jar
And begins to impeccably play Mozart's sorrowful "Requiem"
The music bounces off every wall of the subway car
Before landing on the laps of its occupants

An impossible subway car silence commences
One that I have never experienced before today
This is the kind of moment that can only happen in New York
The violinist plays with the fever and passion
Reminiscent of Joshua Bell's debut at Carnegie Hall
Instinctively, I pull my journal out and begin
Moving my pen across the page
Writing to the pace of the music
Detailing every moment as it unfolds
You eagerly take out your sketchbook
The one you bought in the Village
When we were with Rebecca and Eliot at the NYU art show
I pause my own writing to observe your slender
Almost elegant fingers grip the colored pencil
That replicates the jawline of the violinist to perfection
Your hands are exquisite just like the rest of you
I grow excited at what your sketch might blossom into
The red pencil in your drawing hand
Adds color and detail to the base of the instrument
To the surrounding graffiti clad walls
After a few minutes my pen begins moving again
It imagines this man's story
Did he study at Julliard?
Did he play with the New York City Philharmonic?
Was it one or several twists of fate
That moved his home permanently to the streets?
When he entered the subway car
He looked like just another homeless dweller
But now, watching him play, his face is alive
Color has seeped back into his cheeks
Passion pours from his bow
To the strings of his instrument
I write a paragraph about artists
How they never lose their art
Even when faced with the cruelest of hardships
It is the one thing they can count on to always be there
All of this reminds me of our symbiotic

Friendship that fills our cups to the brim
With eternal, platonic love
The kind that Hemingway and Fitzgerald secretly craved
Beyond their necessary complementary pairing
When the train reaches the Union Square stop
We ascend the stairs to 14th Street
I ask how much you tipped the violinist
You look down at the sidewalk
With a faint sense of unease and utter, "Fifty"
Barely audible above the sounds of the midday traffic
I smile and playfully tip the brim
Of your fedora hat, causing it to fall
I catch it before it hits the ground
Placing your hat on my head
It looks ridiculous on me
Makes us both laugh
Suddenly, you swipe the hat from my head and take off
Running with it in the direction of our destination:
The Strand Book Store
Where our mission today is to find other rare books
To add to the bookcase we share in SoHo

Sea of Nothing

"You're not enough to make me stay."

These words of yours haunt me
Until my heavy eyelids succumb to sleep

I dream I am in the tub underwater
Staring up at the ceiling
I can hear drops of water
Splashing from the faucet
Its sound is muffled and slow
Patiently I wait for each drop to fall
Slower and slower
Like a clock winding to a stop
I can hear its cadence
Feel its vibration
Shaking my sight
Rippling the water
It is insistent and alarming
Like a phone call in the dead of night
Then I realize that this sound I hear
Is my heartbeat
I can feel it in my chest
In my wrists
In my temples
It's the only thing keeping me alive
What's to stop this minuscule mass
From giving out?
I panic and break the surface
Frantically inhaling air back into my lungs
While watching your words
Which once held so much meaning
Disintegrate
Before my eyes
Into a sea of nothing

The Things that Define a Beautiful Moment

Your townhouse is much nicer than ours
It is airy with a large balcony and lots of art scattered throughout
We study on the couch in the living room
Our binders are spread out over the treasure chest coffee table
The couch is mustard gold, and it is old and sinks when we sit
Which means your waist is pressed right into mine
And our knees sometimes touch
But I am not freaking out as much as I expected
I try to play it cool with you, keep my cool with you
The mysterious senior who lives across the street
The one who gives me rides to campus on bad weather days
The one who looks like a heartthrob, but still sees me
The one who plays second singles on the JMU tennis team
The one giving me intimate college algebra lessons
Because I don't know the difference between rise and run on a math graph
The room is floating and golden
It glows honey yellow and nectarine orange
The warmest, most inviting colors
I melt into the whole thing
My sweaty fingers clutch the pencil as I attempt to solve an equation
But instead of focusing on what x equals
I think about how someday I will romanticize this moment
I won't remember the sweat dripping down the back of my neck
I won't remember how nervous I got
Each time your hand innocently grazed mine
I don't want such things to define a beautiful moment
Life is not about that
It is about how people see you
Because the minute they do
Everything else fades away

Ash

My desire for you does not go out
Like a worn-out candle wick
It extinguishes little by little
But continues to burn meticulously
Until all that is left is ash

Believing in the Impossible

I am not in love with you anymore
It's an emotional relief
You smell the same
Mentos and apples
A hint of old baseballs
You sound the same too
Gentle and funny
With the same slight Spanish accent
But I don't get that feeling
I don't think about kissing you
I am not fixated on your green eyes
Or your curly hair
I am cured

Eric and Seth are playing their acoustic set on stage
They're playing a cover of "Wonderwall"
I am supposed to join them and sing harmony
When they close the set with "American Pie"
I have heard this cover of "Wonderwall" before
Seth played it for me in his garage
It sounds even better than I remember
I take a photo and text it to Alicia since she had to work tonight
I turn off my phone and get lost in the music
I move close to the speakers, so thought is impossible
I yell with the crowd when the song finishes
Before joining Eric and Seth on stage for "American Pie"
It feels so good to sing in front of a crowd again
Although, I am not really singing to everyone
 I am singing to the seventh person back from the stage
I am singing to you and your honest eyes that lock with mine I
watch you fidget and lift your baseball cap up and down
As your tongue plays with your upper lip
Your body is nervous but your eyes are not
It is almost as if we are stalled in time

Traveling back to when our love
Was real and tangible
For the entirety of the song
It is you and me
The way we used to be
Looking at one other
As if nothing else matters
Once the song ends, Eric and Seth walk off stage and I follow
I watch as they warmly greet their girlfriends
Who have been watching the show from the side of the stage
I linger there before walking back over
To where Justin is standing
"He misses you, you know," Justin says
Opening and closing his hands
To imitate your mouth
Going on and on about me.
I like the thought of you missing me
I like the thought of you
Telling Justin you miss me
"You still like him, I know you do," Justin adds
And it doesn't make me angry like it did last month
It doesn't hurt, it doesn't hit home
So why can't I stop looking at you
Standing to Justin's left?
Why can't I stop believing
In the impossible and us?

Slipping Through My Fingers

The clock on the wall is blurry tonight
Drops of water fall to the floor in slow motion
From the shirt you hold in your hand
The muscles in your back handcuff my eyes and won't let go
The 8-train rumbles by
Miscellaneous memories hung on the wall sing along
I am glad it's loud enough to drown out my jagged breathing
I take a step forward, unsure of what to do
You glance over your shoulder and ask what I am thinking
I turn as red as a Jersey tomato
Because what I am thinking about is what you wear to bed
What you look like at dawn when the New York sun awakes you
What the stubble on your chin will feel like on my neck in the morning
I am disarmed
You turn and run your index finger down my face to my lips
I move in to kiss you, but you pull back hesitantly
Wanting to know what I am thinking
Wanting to know how it feels to be this close to you
I cannot utter a word because I don't even know myself
When I don't answer you
You playfully hit me with your shirt
And suddenly
The atmosphere in the room becomes silent
I have never seen you without your bravado
It makes you look innocent
It makes you look vulnerable
It commands me to wrap my arms around you
Until the night slips through my fingers

"Just Like the White Winged Dove"

I look over and see you
Neon-green sneakers on the dash
Humming to Stevie
I imagine you at Tavern on the Green
With Diana, holding out
Your scroll copy of *On the Road*
Trying to get up the courage to give it to her
You probably wrote a speech beforehand
And you studied it on the subway ride there
I know you worked out exactly
When her shift would be ending
So you could talk to her without interruption
What you didn't know was that
She was already in love with you
I wish you could have lived
Long enough to have had
Someone like Diana
To love you

You and I didn't tell each other
Everything
But I thought I knew most
Things about you
I thought I knew
The important things
Giving away your beloved scroll
Feels like one of those
I could be sad about this
But at least she still has it
I asked her when we spoke recently
It bothered me that I couldn't
Find it after you died
I looked everywhere
Now it all makes sense

You wanted her to have a part of you
Before your gift of eternal love
We didn't talk much about Diana
Your love for her
Was an intimate secret kept from me
It was something not ready
To be unveiled
I understood that
As I understood you
But why the scroll, Derek?
This is unbelievably selfish of me
To say out loud
But I wish I had it instead of her
I wish so hard that the car jerks
I turn up the music
The next song
Is "Edge of Seventeen"
One of your favorites
When the chorus comes on
I start singing the words
Like you would have done
If you were really here
With your feet up on the dash

It surprises me for a second
I think I hear you say something
About me being as weird as you
Then in my head
You start singing too

Intimate Mixture

Once the front door shuts
The silence is heavy enough
To make my knees buckle
Your scent
An intimate mixture
Of peppermint and sweat
Is all I am left with now

A Burst of Blue

I am in love with the expansiveness of the world
I am in love with everyone
It is almost akin to following a trail of blue crystal beads
The view of something that I know is more evenly pronounced and palpable
It is the pulsating ground reverberating and rebounding up to the birth
Of my true self
This meadow draped in stillness is waiting patiently
Coated in enchantment
Dominated by waves of bending Spanish blue bells
Reserved solely for the purpose of today

Backroom Heartbeat

He walks along the shore at dusk
Up above, gulls ride the breeze over the water
The final rays of the day have turned it gold
Buttery sunlight flashes off the sea
Dancing lambently across his features like diamonds

He arrives at the house
And climbs the steps to the deck
Through the sliding glass door, he sees them
Sitting sideways in a recliner
Legs thrown over one of the arms
Discarded clothing lies on the floor below
The temperate sounds of LL Cool J's "I Need Love"
Waft from the stereo out onto the deck
He recognizes the other man
From their favorite restaurant
Betrayal slithers like a snake around his neck
He descends the stairs

The Ongoing Painful Image

Whenever someone
Mentions your name
My eyes close
Visions of you with him
Assault me

My First Time for the Last Time

We take the shortcut
Through Central Park
The sprinklers are on and we rest near one
Holding our legs over the soft sprays of water
You point to the streetlight and the moths flying around it
They look just like a golden storm
I glance over at you while you are looking up
There is a dusting of faded freckles
On the left side of your face
Running down your neck
Disappearing under your collar
Why am I just noticing these now?
We take off our shoes and socks
To feel the water on our feet
You point at the way
The water reflects on the grass
The blackbird sings at night
The shadows of high-rise buildings
As if picking up the most beautiful parts of the world
And showing them to me for the first time
You explain how the moths use the moon as a guide
Flying toward it
But they never reach it
Because they hit the light down here
Thinking it is the moon

We sit here for a long time
Talking about the unusual things
We want to see
Like the midnight sun, and its opposite, the polar night
And the light reflecting off the sea and snow
Coating everything in blue

The time we spend together

In the weeks leading up
To the end of September
Is beautiful and thick with meaning

After your funeral
I write about
How cruel it is
That a month before you died
You thought so much
About the life you wanted to have

Back to the Bar

I think the bartender approves
Because when we walk in together
He winks

After we order beers
He brings us a round of shots
"These are on the house," he offers
Before grimacing and nodding to his left
To where my ex sits
With that same pretentious fucker
The one from Columbia Law with the white teeth
I roll my eyes and down the lemon drop
You down yours too

After three beers and another round of shots
You're drunk and I need to get you home

I see my ex
He is on the other side of the bar
Watching the two of us leave together
He has been looking at me longingly all night

It is interesting to me
How I look more attractive to him
The second I am with someone else

Outside
The night is still warm
The heat is trapped in concrete and sky
You lean on my shoulder with all your weight
We make it as far as the bench across the street

When you look over
Your eyes are so bloodshot

They look like two cherries
In a glass of milk
You keep opening and shutting your right eye
As if trying to get a clear picture of me
Until you decide to leave the bench
To lie on the sidewalk
"I just need to rest a while," you explain
While gazing up at me, patting the concrete

I lie next to you
Your arm touches mine
And I let myself think
How good it is to be with someone again

I lose all sense of time
Lying here with you on the sidewalk
With the cars moving past

I know it is time to get up
Once you start singing Coldplay
Your lyrics to "Fix You" drop drunk and heavy
Allowing me to see it all
A raining world
A hiding sun
A person fighting to love
Stuck in reverse

I pull you back up on your feet
And ask you to start the song over
This time I join in
Because there is something in it
I need to find
An answer, maybe
To how it is done
How a person finds their worth again

I don't find it, though

All the song does is make me ache

I feel the urge to tell you all of this
Every detail
Of how
Instead of moving on with my life
I have been home rereading *Wuthering Heights*
Hoping Heathcliff gets another chance from Kathy

But you're too drunk tonight
For me to explain any of this
So I am left settling
For the warm feeling
Of your drunk, slender body
Leaning against me

Not a Match

I see you with him
Sitting side by side together
In chairs beside the pool table
You are holding hands
Looking at him
The way you looked at me that first night
Completely focused
Leaning close
You look gorgeous
Brushing strands of dark brown hair from your eyes
This sweeping hand movement of yours
Still drives me crazy
I hate that it does
He looks gorgeous too
The fucker
The lights are picking up and reflecting
The whiteness of his teeth and making his blond hair
Look extra shiny
He is well dressed
I bet he has paid for everything tonight
According to the bartender
He and his white teeth have a life plan
Because he just finished his last year at Columbia Law
I see myself in the mirror
That runs along the back of the bar
My face looks tired
Worn and defeated
The bartender pours me another beer and says:
"For what it's worth, I never thought you two were a match."

The Despair of Your Absence

I spend my twilights here
Out on the deck we used to share
Watching the water, the horizon
The silent, steadfast Palmetto trees

I look down at the stitching
That holds this tattered journal together
And the irony is not lost on me

For the last three weeks
I have been writing
About when you were stained on me
And I was stained on you
Because it helps assuage
My despair
Over your absence

Carnal Tension

Carnal tension thickens the air
As an endless expanse of silence
Eats up more and more time
The gleam in your eyes
Is borderline flirtatious
I can't look away
Neither of us move
But when you lick your lips
I catch myself following the action
Maybe I'm not the only one
 Swarmed with an onslaught
Of unexpected feelings tonight

Pink Champagne

This is the eleventh time
I have been a groomsman
I am happy for Carl and Tracy
I really am, but I dread today
This old southern planation home
Is on a rise overlooking the ocean
Tables are situated all around the dance floor
On top of each table are white linen tablecloths
Silver candles and gold glitter that also dusts the floor
Past the dance floor there are four sets of French doors
That open onto the shore, giving the whole room a fresh, airy feel
The room is full of the other groomsmen in tuxedos
Bridesmaids in peach taffeta
Moving among us are waiters and waitresses
In their black attire carrying drinks on silver trays
A fountain near the French doors spouts pink champagne
What is this, Hotel California?
Organ music fills the room with its elongated, dramatic notes
My face holds only traces of unease and sadness
About being here at another wedding
Playing another intimate role in something
I can never have
The anxiety is so intense in my heart
That this occasion feels harrowing instead of joyful
Playing with the blue sea glass in my pocket
I close my eyes and wish for an escape route out of here,
But when my wish doesn't come true
I take my seat at the head table
I scan the room
Consciously concentrating on each person in succession
To determine if there is anyone here
Who wants to escape too, perhaps even with me
Then I spot you in navy blue, looking bored and unamused
I walk over to you, quietly introducing myself

You look at me suspiciously
Lighting a cigarette with a gold lighter
That is engraved with the initials T. A. R.
A dot of gold is on the top of your left cheekbone
I feel high from the champagne
As I wet my index finger
To remove the gold glitter from your cheek
"What is up with all of this glitter?" you say
While rolling your eyes
I grab two more flutes of champagne from the waiter's tray
And hand one of them to you
Together, we walk up a few steps
To stand just inside the French doors that open onto the veranda
With the shore stretching beyond
So we can look down upon the crowd
We watch the couples dancing, drinking, and laughing
The entire scene is colorful and playful
But up here with us it is imbued with melancholy
I can't tell if it is really there or if I am projecting
My own emotions over to you
"Are you happy to be here?" I ask
Surprised to find myself speaking aloud
"Is it that obvious?" you say
Pulling out another cigarette
Your stature and self-confidence are impressive
It makes you appear sturdy
Your sandy blond hair shines under the lights
Any composure I had before has fled
You offer me your hand and we bound down the stairs
Pushing our way through the crowd
Past sequins and linens and bowties
The bodies recede and lose dimension
Until they are only cutouts from a stage set
Their voices and laughter come in slow recorded warbles
You and I are alone amid this sigh of intimacy
All I can see is your face
Gentle strains of a violin

Float past us like butterflies and sunbeams
As we stand on the balcony with our champagne
The setting sun is turning a majestic cloud formation tangerine yellow
The glinting sea is a brilliant shade of orange sherbet
Dusk has pared down its edges for us
So this little world we share now
Can be tender and memorable

My Day of Love

In my day of love
I saw gold dust spilling
Across the hammock
That hung above a field of goldenrod
Monarch butterflies
Shuddered over our glowing
Intertwined bodies
As bliss rushed through you and me

Magnet and Steel

You are bonded to me
Like magnet and steel
You appear to me in the first light of dawn
Urgently in the forward direction
Like water rushing, time stopping still
Time has receded
Those distances of space and time do not exist
When I hear the catch in your throat
I am reminded of the first caress of our love
Concern rises with the weight of the day
Doors open wide like lips parting
Ready to cradle your tears
With the purest platonic love, I ask
"Do you need my help honoring your brother, Mark, today?"

Pink Champagne II

I am already at the sand's edge
When I see a young couple
Holding hands by the water
I scoff and roll my eyes
And head in the opposite direction
Suddenly, I hear my name
I turn to find you running
Across the expanse of the beach
With a bottle of pink champagne
Fireflies flash like sequins in the dark
"Wait up! I'm coming with you," you say
I want to be alone, but I am unable to say no to you
I watch as you loosen your shirt
And then half-squat, the bottle between your legs
You struggle with the cork
Until it gives way with a loud pop
I duck as it rockets past me toward the water
You offer me the bottle
Foam overflowing onto my hand
The shoreline is silvered
By the brightness of the moon
I try walking with my head back
So I can see the host of stars above
But the motion makes me dizzy
And I collide with you
Our legs tangle
You pull yourself out of it
Without tripping, but I am not as lucky
Looking down, you run your hand
Through your hair
Sitting down next to me
We both take long swallows
From the champagne
That sits beside us in a niche in the sand

We take our shoes and socks off
For a while we walk
Right where the water breaks, without talking
Holding the bottle to my lips
I look at you sideways, smiling
We stop and look at the dark sea
Then up and down
The empty length of the beach, debating
We undress under the cold light of the moon
Before wading out
To where the cool water touches our thighs
Then we dive in
The coldness surprises our hearts
Submerged, we cut through the murkiness
Which is scarier because of the nighttime
To where it is deeper
I can hear my heart beating
It makes me feel strong
Once I reach the surface, I swipe at my eyes
Trying to orient myself
When I get my bearings, all I see are your eyes
They're closing and then your lips
Touch mine

Thanks for…

When I open the door
You are standing there
In a navy-blue windbreaker
Blue for me because you know
It is my favorite color
You wrap your arms tightly
Around my neck
I feel a little suffocated
But it is exactly what I need right now
Once we break apart
I lean my forehead to yours
We shut our eyes and stay this way
For many heartbeats
Until you give me a limpid look
The green of your eyes catches the light
At just the right angle
They become translucent
And depthless
I am forcibly pulled into them
Feeling like I am being sucked in
Deeper and deeper
By an undertow
Until there is nothing
But green
The salty evening air is chilly
The wood of the porch
Is cold beneath our feet
The surf rolls in the distance
The wind hisses
Seething through
The willow's boughs
A mist descends on us
As you put your arms
Around me from behind

Nuzzling your head on my neck
Your long hair is soft
Against my skin
I rest my hands
On your forearms
Leaning back into your strength
I breathe deeply and whisper
This vocal ellipsis
"Thanks for…"
The wind blows the rest
Of my words away
For a moment I wonder
If I have even spoken at all
Then you whisper back, "Always."
Sighing into my hair

Pink Champagne III

Thoughts of you and me
Echo dully in the underwater
Chamber of my head
They are hard to pin down
Despite seeming to come
More slowly than I am thinking them
I try to focus on them, process them
How I pushed you away
For going too fast and too hard
And how your face looked amid my rejection
When suddenly it seems I have been immersed forever
The ticking clock of my heart is winding down
I become frantic, fearful my lungs will burst
I struggle to the surface
Breaking into the atmosphere
With the desperation of one
Caught in an undertow
The taunting thoughts
Of my painful breathing
Releases simultaneously
I pant for air
When I get my bearings, I see
That you are already cutting through the surf
With sure, even strokes toward the shore
By the time I reach the sand
You are seated by our clothes
You're trying to find your second sock
Your lips are pursed
You don't look up as I approach
Your skin is fraught with goosebumps
In the suddenly crisp night
Blond locks are pasted to your forehead
Your hair is matted with saltwater
"I better go," you frown

Running a hand through your sopping hair
I plop into the sand
We sit for a few minutes
Passing the bottle
Without looking at each other
Our bare legs touching
You cock your head to look at me with an open, pained face
I am surprised to see your vulnerability
You bring your knees up, hugging them to your chest
Biting your bottom lip hard, you begin to cry
Your tears opalescent in the moonlight
I don't know what to think or what to say
I put an arm around your shoulders
You lean into my chest
After your cries cease
You look up and say, "I'm so sorry."
Sounding remarkably sincere
You stand
Your emotions seemingly have run dry
You begin to dress
I do the same
As I pull on my clothes, I watch you
You catch me looking and smile
An embarrassed, self-conscious smile
And say, "Don't look at me, I feel stupid."
We finish dressing without speaking
The night wind off the sea is stiff and cool
The empty champagne bottle
Dangles from your hand
Even the sea grazing the shore is quiet
"Do you resent me, now?" you ask in a tentative voice
"No, of course not," I say a little too quickly
But deep down, we both know
There is no way to make this right
The script has already been written

So Insignificant

He sits alone
Looking at the water
Listening to it, breathing it in
A subtle breeze arouses
The waning leaves on the trees
The boat docked beside him
Sways with the rhythm of the waves
Its ropes groaning in protest
He looks up at the moon
Its coy half face mocking him
Just as your words did one hour earlier
When you bit the right side of your lip and said,
"I tried hard to love you, Robert, I really did."

Fifty Years

Now with the decades
Stacked up underneath me
Like library books
I see the beauty of finding freedom
In the refuge of an open heart with no destination
And in notebooks waiting to be filled
With short stories and poetry

Washington, D.C.

By the time we reach the National Mall
The morning haze has burned off

We relax on the lawn
Lying on our backs
Eyes shut to the glow of the sun
The day is warm, and it makes us lazy
And we both drift off for a bit.

The rain wakes us, though
We hop up
Hastily collecting our belongings
And bolt to the car

Your face is shiny with rain
Our breath is hard and loud
Under the torrential downpour
You are holding your fogged
Glasses in one hand
Your hair hangs in strands
All around your shoulders

You are beautiful

The rain hammers the car roof
And then it stops
Just like that

The sudden silence is louder
Than the rainstorm had been

We both look out the window in surprise
Then I turn to you, smiling
Your eyes are focused upward

As bright as the sky
"I am looking for the rainbow," you explain
"I feel cheated!"

The Magic Hill

Today is not a beach day
Since the sky is the color of pewter

We ride our rented bikes
To Cape May Point
To a majestic hill
Covered in purple heather
That stretches up to the ashen sky
Dandelions dot the hillside
Their bright yellows contrast
With the violet resplendence

You let your bike fall
To the side of the path, your mouth agape
"I knew you would love it here" I say
"I call it the magic hill."
"Last one to the top buys dinner?" you ask
Wearing a mischievous grin
Bees and butterflies flit about, oblivious
As we race each other up the hill
At the top, the clouds are nearer and bigger
More tangible than before
The wind whistles around us and through our hair
Playfully, you fall into the flowers, feigning exhaustion
Purple petals cling to your disheveled hair
I lay beside you, catching my breath
Thinking about everything I like about you
Like how you breathe into me when we kiss
The way you say my name
Your smile and your camera and your superstitions
Music even sounds different since you

Here
Surrounded by violet blossoms

You have never looked more beautiful
"I feel like I am touching infinity'" you exclaim
Nodding my head in agreement and lowering my face
I brush the hair away from your lips
So we can breathe into one another again
As we kiss

Tender at Dusk

We reach the boardwalk
Just as the setting sun
Is turning the regal clouds and shimmering sea
A brilliant shade of orange

I love how the world always feels more tender at dusk

The proximity of you drowns out everything
The Springsteen cover band, the people, even the ocean
Points of light catch in your eyes as they investigate mine
And they flash as if lit from within
Dimensionless, like a cat's
Allowing me to see into them, into you
Your hair shifts in the wind
"Look," you say, pointing to the dimming sky
I look up to see the first star burning
Through the kaleidoscopic rush of sunset
I close my eyes and make a wish
"What did you wish for?" you ask
Your face lit deeply in pink by the parting sun
I squint back at you and say, "How did you know I made a wish?"
"Because I did too!" You say
With your I'm-so-high-I-can't-stop-smiling look
The one that always makes me laugh
Then, as if on cue, the cover band segues
Into Springsteen's "Secret Garden"
And all I want to do is slow dance with you

This Place with You

Like a movie reel inside my head
A sequence of images from earlier in the day
Play over and over
I had been standing in the water
Looking back at you on the shore
With your camera aimed at me
My face so vividly expressed my feelings
Were you able to see the lovesick glint in my eye?
And worse, could you see my sadness?
I have never been able to hide my emotions
But I hadn't realized just how clearly
They were telegraphed
Until I saw those photos you took
Tonight, as I look out at the roaring sea
I cannot stop thinking of your reaction
To having your own picture taken
When I grabbed your camera on the beach
I noticed how your amusement turned to horror
You put your hand over your face shyly
Explaining that you were just the man behind the lens
I didn't expect this reaction from you
But I understood why
No one has ever made you feel special
I want to be the one to make you finally see
How special you are
I hope I get the chance
I am so captivated by you
That it keeps my sadness at bay

I smile at the memory of our dinner last night
When your foot innocently bumped mine
All I could concentrate on
Was the small point of pressure
It was insanely intimate

Hot energy coursed through my veins
Stimulating my cells, kindling my passion
You and I both looked up
Unable to keep from smiling and laughing
I want more moments like this
Because I am happy here with you
In this place I love the most
But this happiness is sharp and poignant
And reminds me of sadness
Because I cannot share it with anyone, let alone you
The one person who does understand
Without the fear of losing you

Sleeping on the Right Side

I want to stay up until the wee hours
Discussing how special you are
This is the thought I have
As you and I make up our beds on the floor
Although it is unseasonably warm
It is still weeks before Memorial Day
And the official start of the beach season
So none of the bedrooms in this house
Are ready for occupants
I watch as you slip into your sleeping bag
I try not to stare
At your cute yellow Superman pajama bottoms
You tell me that you don't mean to be rude
About turning your back on me while sleeping
You don't like sleeping on your left side
Because that's the side the heart is on
And it creeps you out to know that gravity
Is pulling everything else on top of it
All of this leaves me a bit speechless
You look at me again and apologize for "being weird"
I smile back and wink, "It's okay, I like weird."
Your eyes do that thing that I love
They grow bigger and hold their blink
It lets me know you approve
I place my E. Lynn Harris book on the nightstand
And turn off the light
Before lying on my own right side
My head rests on my hand
In the sudden darkness
I don't see your slumbering form at first
Then it abruptly becomes visible
I fixate on the rise and fall of your chest
It's even and slow
For a few moments I gaze at the silhouette of you

The one who has erased so much of my pain
Then, closing my eyes, I listen to your breathing
It sounds like a series of light sighs
I listen for a long time
Dreaming about making you sigh like this
For me in the waking hours
Before I allow myself to drift off to sleep
I awake at 4:00 a.m.
An hour that is not
The night and not the morning
It is an hour that doesn't belong anywhere
For me, this is the darkest hour
I have been awake for a few seconds
And cannot shake the feeling of falling
It takes another second to figure out where I am
Because I am not used to being on the floor
Once the world rights itself, I can finally focus
But I am startled to find your face
Only inches from my own
You have turned over in your sleep
My heart pounds at the proximity
There is something so extraordinarily sexy
About the way your dark brown hair drapes over your face
I don't breathe for fear of waking you
I lay still, trying to control my heartbeat
As I wait for the violet and blue morning to arrive

Our Plan to Make James Dean Jealous

We arrive at Myskyns Tavern just in time
For the Jeffrey Gaines show
I had to drag you out tonight
But you seem happy that I did now that we are here
We are greeted by Scott, our bartender friend
Who slides us the two frosted mugs
Of Rolling Rock he poured when he saw us walk in
Before waving over the security guard
Who has saved us two places in front of the stage
I see him before you do
He is wearing a cool denim jean jacket
The way his blond hair is combed back
Makes him look a lot like a 1990s version of James Dean
I suppose I get why you are so attracted to him
And why you so desperately want him back
My guess is that he is here tonight
To make sure you see him
Since I find it hard to believe that this Nirvana-obsessed guy
Is here for the folky
Poetic sounds of Jeffrey Gaines
The second he spots us, he turns
And throws us a puzzled gaze
I lock eyes with him and whisper to you, "It's time!"
Time to set our plan in motion
I tell you to relax, but I am one to talk
Since I cannot even heed my own advice
Because all I can think about
Is kissing your full, luscious lips
The same lips I have been curious about
Ever since we met and became friends
So, yeah, I am doing this
To make "James Dean" jealous
But another part of me wants to savor your lips
To have you kiss me back

It is a great kiss
The first kiss I have really felt
For a long time
I would be lying if I said
I didn't feel it in all sorts of places
I keep my eyes closed, but the light
Seems to have slipped under my eyelids
Because there is a lightning show
Happening in there amid the darkness
My thoughts play like a medley in my head
In no particular order
Why on earth would he keep leaving someone
Who kisses like this?
Derek should be here now to see this
I need his play-by-play recap
What are you thinking?
Damn, your lips are soft!
They are as soft as my pillow
Is this kiss going to make things awkward
Between us now?
You're kissing me back, hard
But is this just you acting the part
Or are you turned on too?
When should we stop?
Should I slow down and hold your face?
Or is that a bit much?
I kind of wish you still had
A few M&Ms in your mouth
So you can pass them over to me as we kiss
Is that gross?
Is your body shaking or is that mine?
Is it bad that the thought
Of kissing you all night appeals to me?
I pull away first and try to read your expression
You look confused, thrilled, worried
All three perhaps
"Is he still watching?" I ask

"Yes," you say, and I can feel
Your breath as you answer
It wears the scent of Rolling Rock beer and M&Ms
"You'll have him back within the week," I tell you
With a nod and wink
While trying my best
Not to sound unhappy

Scene From a Best Friendship

The room is lit by the falling snow outside
The blinds are cracked open
The large flakes have caught the light
Streaming right across the room

I can't sleep
I should be exhausted
But my eyes won't stay closed

Even the peaceful silence
Does little to lull me

I count every breath you take
Thinking about how
In this great big world
Most never find the people they're looking for
Some look all their lives
For the one person
Who understands their heart the best
I am lucky to have found you
The king who holds
The other half of my heart

The Simple Act of Directing Your Eyes

The stress of the day
Doesn't live in my brain for long
Once you get in the car

We sit there silently
Looking at each other
Listening to the blended voices
Of Billie Eilish and Khalid
Stream from the radio
While in the back of my head
I wonder why it is
That I like looking at you so much
The simple act of directing your eyes at somebody else
Shouldn't be all-consuming, should it?
Well, perhaps it should

Missed Opportunity

We were strangers
Sitting side by side
On a New York train that afternoon
When I felt you turn your head
And focus on these words I was writing in my journal:
"I'd rather spend my time earning the right to know a person."
Your eyes flickered up to mine for the briefest of seconds
You nodded your head slowly in agreement
Before looking away

For a moment
It was as if a heavy curtain had fallen around us
The outside noise of the moving train was gone
It was just you and me
The rest of the world's clamor faded
Into the only sound I could hear
The erratic beat of my own heart

Nick and Rob

We didn't know that one day
We wouldn't be eighteen anymore
We didn't know that youth doesn't last
For it is only a moment
Before it disappears
By the time you realize it
It's too late
It's finished
Vanished
Lost
I can still sense it
All of it

Maybe it was our quirkiness
Or the music we liked
That brought us together
On that first day of college
Making us lifelong friends

I laugh whenever I think about visiting Mary T.
Over at her dorm on Friday nights
At very unreasonable hours
Hanging out downstairs
In the large piano room
We loved sliding across the freshly polished floor in our socks
Racing each other to the wall
Sometimes playing "Heart and Soul"
Loudly on the piano
Until the RA kicked us out

Tonight
The music you loved so much
Plays on repeat in my ears
Taking me back

To the shores of our youth

I add deep regret
To the tears I shed in the rain
But there is comfort
Knowing that every time I play these songs
I hear your voice
Recognize your laughter
And see those piercing blue eyes
Tearing in the wind
As we walk together
Across the Quad
One last time

The Epiphany

I used to tell myself
That in the moment you stay for me, I'll know
But there isn't any hope of that ever happening
Now that you have left me here again
I'll count the stars on my own

As I lie awake tonight
Staring up at the intricate patterns
Of the ceiling tiles
I think about my coming of age
In my hometown of Westfield, NJ
Reminiscing about when I was a kid
Chubby and unafraid
When the world seemed
Like it was blissfully endless
But everything made sense
And all of it was in its right place
I think about what I wanted back then
And what I want now
And where those things intersect
Maybe my sweet spot is right here
Within the tender insistence
Of the Stevie Nicks song
Playing on my Beats by Dr. Dre headphones
Or in the pulsating touch
Of the one who is destined
To love me the most

Sherry Darling

Derek and I take the L-train
To the 1, and exit Christopher Street station
To the madness of its intersecting streets
And hordes of partiers on the prowl
Derek nods his head in approval at the six foot five drag queen
Floating past us in her six-inch stilettos
We both love this neighborhood
For its interesting mixture of artistic expressions
Once we arrive at Chumley's, it is already packed
With men and women conducting New York-style debates
In battered wooden booths
Derek and I squeeze into an open spot by the bar
Facing a picture of Dylan Thomas
Among other portraits of dead authors and vintage book jackets
The yesteryear atmosphere soaked in soft yellow-orange lighting
Feels soothingly permanent in this place
Where Hemingway and Fitzgerald once shared drinks
Back when it hosted primarily literary types
These days, the crowd is a mixture
Of young metropolitans, students, and artsy types
Derek orders shoestring potatoes for us to share
And two mugs of Samuel Adams Summer Ale
As I scribble in a pocket-sized spiral notebook
Cramming words in margin to margin as tidy as possible
"What are you writing?" Derek asks
"Just getting down the details of our day so far," I respond
Without looking up
"Of course you are, sire!" Derek says
While arching a dubious eyebrow
At the Winona Ryder/River Phoenix cloned couple passing by
"Are you recording these two posers too?" Derek asks sarcastically
"No, but I will
I have been busy writing about
Jason Priestly and Luke Perry over there," I say

Motioning to the bar where two young men are gesturing
To a group of pretty girls in floral Courtney Love baby doll dresses
I write about our unapologetic originality
My offbeat quirkiness and Derek's effortless polished style
In my notebook before placing it back in my pocket
When Springsteen's "Sherry Darling" comes on
We pause
The entire room is singing along
To the matter of Bruce's desire
To escape the sweltering city streets with Sherry
Down a free, open highway
I feel a swelling in my chest
A surge of joy in my veins
There is nothing like singing in a group
To a chorus of a song that embodies the essence
Of a New York summer dream
Our voices rebound from every corner
Declaring to the world that we are young and free
And that the future stretches out endlessly before us
Like the New York highway in Springsteen's song

Ledges Seem to Be Our Thing

I find you outside the Sistine Chapel
Leaning against a motorcycle
I compliment you on finding
Such a badass vehicle to stand near
And look cool up against
You laugh and say, "No, this is mine."
I gawk and reply, "I'm not getting on that!"

Now we are standing
In the grand foyer of the Vatican
The ceilings are curved high
Made of fine, Italian marble
Frescos abound
It feels like we are at the center
Of the Italian universe

As I wait for you to return with our tickets
I realize that every little thing
I have done this morning feels significant
It is like a lonely, intimate, journal entry
You and I walk out to a large terrace
The area has massive sculptures
This is the hottest day
I have ever experienced in Rome
The sun is relentless
I rest back against a ledge
As you take in the sculptures
You lean next to me
I smile at how ledges seem to be our thing
You nudge my waist and lean deeper into my side
Before whispering this phrase in my ear:
"Speak your truth with conviction,
As if revealing your eye color, Rob."
I watch as you jump from the ledge

And take a curtain call bow before me
"It is all in the delivery, Rob."
I smile and wonder
If you have always
Been like this
Confident in yourself
In talking to others
And in putting yourself out there
In a place where "yourself"
Isn't always welcome
But maybe it isn't confidence
Maybe it is assumption

You fascinate me
As I listen to you summarize
The history of this iconic place
I cannot deny our chemistry
Something is setting in
Like the moment paint begins to dry
On a canvas
I think about one day living here
In Rome, with you
This thought feels just as important
As all these statues and painted ceilings
When you grab my arm
And tug me over to the next exhibit
It snaps me from my daydream
My heart races at the feel of your touch
We pass images of ancient Rome
Sewn into the tapestries on the walls
Then I see it, the big red sign
At the top of a forlorn staircase
"This is it," you whisper
Your breath resting on my ear
As we pass through the door
I am expecting the earth to shift
The room is dark and cool

From the AC blowing on high
It is crowded and I am distracted
Until you nudge me
"Look up," you utter
The first thing I see is the Michelangelo image
God and Adam, with their hands reaching out
Fingers barely touching
My eyes ping everywhere
These painted figures are their own world high above
It all comes alive before my eyes

In the most important room in the world
My gaze sweeps around
All the layers and levels of this world
That Michelangelo created
Shows me what humans can accomplish
If their will is strong enough
You brush your hand against mine
For a few seconds, our thumbs link
I look up and take in the designs of the ceilings
And the cool air of the room
Then I take one more look at you
You nudge my arm
And I think to myself:
In this room
Amid the world's
Finest art
I still just want to look at you

Bye

Watching you turn and walk away
As he called out your name
Was when his last tear evaporated

Starless Sky

A few days after you died
I took to poring over the photos
I had taken of you
One by one, the images ripped at me
But I could not stop looking at them
Because part of me feared
They might be all I have left of you

Later, I went to my bookcase
Searching for a mythical escape
I chose *The Little Prince*
A childhood favorite of mine

The story moved quickly as I read
At times I even found myself laughing a little
But by the end, my heart was heavier than before

I stared at the last drawing in the book for a long time
Wanting more than that barren landscape and solitary star
I remember venturing outside and looking up in the sky
Hoping for a constellation
But I saw no stars

Dented Heart

He sits alone
Head in his hands
As the darkness bleeds
Through the sunlit room
Creating walls
With no windows or doors
Around his dented heart

Mr. Randhawa

After my dad died
I never expected
To have another father figure in my life
But then I met you

You were my best friend's dad
A man balanced perfectly
Between sensitive and strong
Just like my own dad

There were so many similarities
Between you and my dad
You lived for your wife
Your children and grandchildren
Putting your own personal needs last

You treated me like your own son
Calling your house my house too

I remember the first time
We spoke at length
You told me how happy you were
That Kai met me
Because in your eyes
We were two
With nearly identical hearts

I loved hearing you talk
About your days as a high school principal
Back in India
Your eyes lit up
You beamed with pride
When you told me how Kai and Navi
Were both valedictorians at your school

How Kai was drawn to the stage
Performing at an early age
While Navi excelled in dancing

You were proud of your military service
Speaking about how it helped shape the man you became
And when I gave you one of my dad's favorite novels to read
The Great Santini by Pat Conroy
You dove right in
Finding Conroy's words
Relatable and riveting

Having Indian afternoon tea
With you and the family
Was a given anytime I visited
I am not a tea drinker
But I do love Indian chai

We laughed at how much
Of your wife's homemade cheese I ate
On my birthday
When I close my eyes
I can still hear laughter echoing in my ears

You took an interest in my writing
Reading my books and discussing your favorites
You told me that I wrote with great clarity
Something lacking, in your opinion, from most poetry

The last time I saw you was on the day you left for India
We drank tea and talked about Navi coming here in July for a visit
You were excited for when we would all be together

I didn't expect the awful news
When Kai called me early Friday morning
To tell me that you had suffered a massive heart attack

I told myself that this couldn't be true
Because I could still hear
Your distinctive voice in my ears

Why do words carry so much more weight
After a loved one is gone?
Is it because they will never say anything else?
Or perhaps it is because the connection is so strong
That it allows us to still hear their voice
Inside our minds

I think you would love knowing
That even though you are gone from this world
Your presence down here is still very much alive

Intimate Silence

We stare out across the empty field
The woodpeckers are back at it
In the trees overhead
The shade cast through the fence is thick
And riddled with tiny holes of light
Which is akin to standing beneath mesh
Staring up into the sky
A single bead of condensation
Glides down the curve of your water bottle
I am tempted to catch it on my fingertip
And say, "Make a wish!"
But that doesn't work for water
There are no wishes to be found in water

Whatever words I may have
For you in this moment
Feel inadequate
When you put your head on my shoulder
And I loop an arm around your back
I realize the power of our intimate silence
Is all that's needed right now

Disdain

You hold onto disdain
Like it's a prize
The last time we spoke
I lied
I'll never be fine

Befuddled

I hear melodies under my skin
I am hungry for the unapologetic love
The kind I thought I would never have
We have absolutely nothing in common
And yet we have everything in common
I can taste you
Even now as you lean against
Your wall covered in Polaroids
Casually strumming random chords
On your guitar
You have me befuddled

Dear Derek (4/4/2021)

I began reading *Wuthering Heights* again tonight and after the first few pages, it made me think about that snowy February day in Central Park with you. We sat on a rock that we had cleared the snow from and watched the sun set until just a few children remained ice skating on Wollman Rink. Earlier in the day, other children rode sleds down the hill or built snowmen and some threw snowballs at one another, which caused at least two children to cry. Neither of us wore a watch, so the only way we could estimate the time was from the sun. I wish we could have spent more days like this together, because inside this moment, it was as if the passage of time didn't exist outside of us, which is the reverse of how things typically feel in New York. The sun made the snow covering the park look rose gold like the clouds at sunset, and the elm trees without branches were reminiscent of the elderly Italian hands of grandpa Cozzi. I wish I had brought the Polaroid so we could have taken a picture together. The fallen snow framed the rink like a Currier and Ives painting as we inhaled the air and listened to the sounds of the children. I opened my journal and wrote about all the different sensations that had penetrated my nonvisual core. I wanted to preserve the emotions by writing them down, but I found it difficult to organize them, so I asked you to close your eyes with me so we could concentrate exclusively on the feeling we received from the cold air that removed all aromas except for a minimal amount of your watermelon-flavored gum. It was still complex to classify it, but we tried anyway.

When we opened our eyes, the sun was almost all the way down. You shook your head, picked up some snow and compressed it with both hands. You laughed, amused I am sure, by your ongoing willingness to indulge me in such ridiculous behaviors for the sake of art. I finished my journal entry and when I looked over, you were still compressing the snow in your hands into a sphere. Your body vibrated from the wind, and you said it was getting late and that we should begin heading back to SoHo. You were about to throw the snowball you held in your glove, but it remained there as we walked in silence to the sub way station until you dropped it outside the escalator where it blended in with all the other snow piled up to the left of the sidewalk. We read the Sunday New York Times on the subway and scoured the book review section for the next book we would read together, deciding on Jacquelyn Mitchard's, *The Deep End of the Ocean* because we liked the sound of the conflicting characters.

That night, we stayed in while it snowed and listened to the new Elliott Smith CD and read *The Great Gatsby* aloud. We discussed how Fitzgerald's sentences were more complex than Steinbeck's. Then we ordered food— our favorite, pad Thai—and lounged in the living room, eating and discussing how effective Nick Carraway's narration was in Gatsby.

This was one of the most enjoyable days that I spent with you in New York that year, Derek, because we did not allow anyone or anything to intrude upon our world. After you had fallen asleep on the floor, resting your head on the oversized red sofa pillow, I covered you up in the afghan I had given you for Christmas, the one I asked my Aunt Betty to make. I envied how you were able to fall asleep peacefully anywhere. The snow was several inches higher on the windowsill and still growing as I thought about this day with you which had felt simultaneously familiar and new, which was a fascinating combination. I remember thinking this is how all experiences should feel or how I should make them feel, but often they feel too familiar, or I desire something solely because it is new. With you, the blending of new and familiar was natural and effortless. With you, I knew what it was like to know that my happiness was making you happy and this feeling was reciprocal, Derek. I miss that.

I began revisiting Gatsby today too, Derek, because Kindra, Rhiannon, and I will be discussing it on an upcoming Instagram live. I plan on bringing the notes we made when we read this together in 1997, so our fascinating combination of familiar and new can live on.

-R

Who We Are and Always Will Be

You are part of my existence, part of myself. You have been in every line I have ever written since. You have been in every possibility I have ever seen—on the beach, on the sails of boats, in the wetlands, in the clouds, in the sidewalk cracks, in the dark, in the light, in the wind, in the trees, in the waves, and in the heat of the sun before it melts away. I love the permanence we have carved together. It's our legacy—our forever—it is who we are and who we will always be. Blue, red, orange, yellow, purple, and gold—our colors—will never fade.

June 21, 2006: Our Last Night at the Beach House

Out past the dunes
Heat lightning glimmers on the water
Tonight, there is just enough breeze
To keep us from being miserable

I sit shirtless on the swing
On this porch by the sea
Balancing James Baldwin's *The Fire Next Time*
And my journal on my lap
You lie on the floor below
Reading Fitzgerald's *The Great Gatsby*
I pause to admire the image of you
Your wind-swept hair
The way you comfortably chew your cheek
As you read
The white tank top you wear
Billows around your slender form
Despite the moistness of the night
You are fresh and dry

When you look up, I flush at being caught
You smile and move up next to me on the swing
So close our faces are almost touching
Over the water we hear a low touch of thunder
You avert your face toward the sea
I go to put my arm around you
But in doing so, I bump your glasses
To a diagonal position on your face
We both laugh and I slide my arm around you
comfortably this time
"It feels so good to laugh with you," you say, leaning in
"Because sometimes I feel like Nick Carraway,
Observing a privileged world I don't belong to or understand
But you understand me, Rob."

I slowly turn to you, comprehending
"I do understand you, I really do."

June 21, 2006: Our Last Night at the Beach House II

As the sun begins to set
Into the bleached horizon
I lean on the rail of the porch
Looking toward the place
Where the sea meets the sky
Then I hear my name
I turn to find you standing
At the door behind me
Looking at me for a long time
As if you are memorizing me
And this last night at the ocean together

We sleep with the windows open
Under the full moon
The ocean's roar can be heard
Off in the distance
I awaken from a light sleep
Slipping out of bed and into my bathing suit
I venture out past the wild grass of the dunes
To the cool, damp sand
I fall into the water's chill
Swimming out past the breakers
To where a light mist hovers
Just above the surface
And immerse myself in the sparkling brine
It takes a moment to get used to
This underwater sound I hear
Because it is the first time
I have been aware of the loud beating of my heart
It is like a drum, insistent as time
I feel it at the pulse points of my wrist
I break the surface and swim
With steady freestyle stokes
Back to shore, back to you

Once home
I snuggle into you
Our legs tangling like roots
Your back settles into my chest
Our hearts aligned
We lie still
Just like this
For the rest of the night

The Cleverly Hidden Secret Treasure

As I write about this love
I adore everything about you
It is how it always was
Do you think about me now?

In the beginning of us
I was in awe
Even walking next to you
I couldn't bear to look at you
It was like God had cleverly hidden
A secret treasure right before my eyes
In the background, the city sung
And I was finally able to compose myself
Enough to look at all that you were
It was like when I snuck a glimpse of you
When you were tending bar
You told me the summer would be different for you
Now that I was back in New York
You said that SoHo New Yorkers
Love their rooftops in summer
When the weather is warm
For a moment, I closed my eyes
And let myself imagine an entire summer
With you and your friends
Building love together
As high as the skyscrapers that surround us at every turn
While traveling deeper into an understanding of it all
Everything is you—fiery, magnetic, original
Memorable, electric, and it stirs
Everything in me

The Shores of Time

Everything is in front of me
They are twins
The bottom one is firm
The upper is bent
Like a breaking wave
I am riding it towards the shores of time
It escapes through tiny crevices
On its way to irrelevance

Every Shade of You

Browns, tans, brick-red, and warm greys abound
Along with the shaded green of baseball diamonds
Turquoise lives in your eyes when you are a haven of peace
But when you are a storm rolling in, colors are muted

I saw nothing but darkened grey
And subdued blue after our separation
You had been the yellow in this relationship
But now you were the shade
Capable of shutting me out
Of your glistening sunlight
Leaving me to seek refuge
In passed-out, blackened sleep
Under pale white covers
Littered with cookie crumbs

Eleven years later, every hue is reawakened
Suddenly, I see greens and yellows again
Earthy tones emanate
From each syllable of your message
White gloved hands
Speckled with dusty brown baseball dirt reach out for mine
With the soft, red delicacy of rose petals

Driving Through the Holland Tunnel with My Eyes Shut

I feel like I have just done something regretful
Like driving through the Holland Tunnel with my eyes shut

My mind replays the image of you
Standing in front of a full-length mirror
Dripping wet
I down my last tequila shot
And watch you undo the towel around your waist
My eyes jump between your body in front of me
The shot glass in my hand
And the whirring ceiling fan above
You take a step forward, brushing your leg against my arm
As if tracing the sexiest word in the dictionary
Then there are mouths, hands, torsos, and motion
That move quickly and precisely
On their way to a familiar crescendo

Afterwards, you insist we go out for falafels
We don't say much to each other
As we zigzag the busy side streets of Chelsea
It is a Friday night, New York is buzzing
We sit at a picnic table outside the Moroccan Café
Which is located just across from the pier
Covered in white outdoor lights
I can hear the faint sound of water
Splashing in the background
You glance up from the menu
I straighten my back, avoiding your gaze
You reach over and tap my wrist
I grip the edges of the menu tighter
Earlier in the night, your touch was all that I wanted
But now your touch feels like a bee sting

I Would Rather Be with You

I am a strange mix of things today
I am spark from your hands
And memory from your lips
I am warmth from your blush
And calm because I am certain
You are mine now and I am yours
Because you took my hand
Held it in a way that let me know
This sounds unreal
But it is the one thing I knew
That was always going to happen
I am sober but I feel drunker than ever
Staring at a spot of air in front of me
On this southbound train
The spot is you, squinting back at me
I am riding higher and higher
Towards love's precipice
Ever since you
The one with the wild, curly brown hair
Offered a hand
At Radio City Music Hall
You looked extremely tall
Because you were standing a step above me
But when you came down
You were only a couple of inches taller
With droopy, kind eyes
The kind that look tired in a cute way
My heart was beating fast again
Just like when Debbie Harry sang "Maria"
During her encore tonight
Then you did something drastic
Something that relieved all the fears
Swirling in my head
You looked away

From the attractive
Blonde woman on your arm
And took a pen from your pocket
Writing on the back of your ticket stub
You held it out as your blue-green eyes
Flickered downward
Our fingers touched and became entwined
Under the strings of lights that hung above
Looking down at the ticket stub, I read your words:
"I would rather be with you."
A smile covered my face
Suddenly, someone taps me on the shoulder
I look up and see Sam, the train conductor
Staring down at me with concern as he says,
"Rob, this is your stop!"
His words end my fantasy of you
But at least you are still mine
When I daydream on a train

Dear Derek (3/28/2021)

Sometimes when I dream about you, it is a detailed echo of a moment we shared.

You and I are back at that bodega on Greene Street, buying two root beer Snapples. We take them to the courtyard behind your building and sit on a bench by the concrete rectangle that darting children and roller hockey players commandeer in the daytime. I have been here by myself dozens of times during the day. It is a good place to write because I love inhaling the laughter and sounds of the kids at play. This courtyard has the feel of an open-air movie set, far away from the clamor of the city. You take large gulps of your Snapple and I nurse mine. You point up to the flock of clouds sweeping over the moon, saying how they resemble a tattered wedding dress. I loved your artistic eyes, Derek.

We drink for a minute without speaking, rinsed in a mild breeze that heightens the sweet decay of the surrounding wet leaves. Silent outdoor experiences like this, in an acre of space without anyone in sight, are rare in New York City. The oak tree branches rattle around us. Late night revelers shout in the distance. The two of us stare straight ahead into the empty play area and swallow a mouthful of our drinks. We have shared countless, memorable jaunts together, but this moment, occupying the stillness in a tranquil pocket of the city night, feels more exciting.

You break the silence and ask, "What is your greatest fear, Rob?" You look at me. "I fear the future because it is something I cannot see," I respond tentatively. "For me, it is the thought of being fully open with the woman I love because I doubt her true intentions," you counter with a similar apprehension.

I remember thinking about how everyone has something they prefer not to think about. Back then, I didn't want to think about my future. Perhaps part of me knew that our time together would be limited so I stayed living inside the present tense. I was not surprised when you revealed that your biggest blind spot was not knowing the true intentions of people. You told me that I was the first real friend that you could confide in after spending a lifetime holding everyone at arm's length, especially women. "Let's go to the river!" you exclaim with the excitement of a spirited child, "it has been forever since I have seen it at night."

We walk through SoHo to the exit at 20th Street and cross over the FDR to the East River. The water stretches ominously across to Greenpoint. We follow the fencing south along the pedestrian path until you stop to finish off your root beer Snapple.

You look at me, blinking your eyes several times before suggesting, "Is it a stupid idea to write our biggest fears in our empty Snapple bottles and throw them in the water? I know you are going to say that it is littering, but just stay with me here, Rob. It is a symbolic gesture. I want us to wake up tomorrow fearless. You game, sire?"

I grin back at you and take out the spiral notepad and pen from my pocket. I hand them to you and turn around so you can use my back to lean on and write. I watch as you fold the paper into your bottle, and then hand the pen and pad over to me. I quickly copy down what I said to you earlier about fearing my future and I drop it in my bottle, which still has some root beer in it. I watch as you fling your bottle over the fence, and I follow suit. As expected, yours travels further than mine. The synchronized splashes pierce the buzzing sound of the highway traffic behind us before the bottles containing our greatest fears sink out of sight forever.

I suppose I have you to thank for my ongoing fearlessness. I saw your fearlessness when you proposed marriage to Diana. She and I spoke last year for the first time since your death, Derek. She sounds happy but I know she misses you too. I don't know if she and I will speak again, but perhaps I will send her the new book once it is finished so she can read keep reading about you. The nights are lonely, but I soldier on, living the life you wanted me to lead. I will never forget this day when, like the "magic man" in that old, classic Heart song, you made my greatest fear disappear forever.

-R

My First Time for the Last Time II

There was something about your shadow on the lawn
That late September night in Central Park
The way the moths flew directly above
The golds and blues in the night flooded you
When I look back now
Reading the past with the present in my eyes
I think about how those last days together
Were beautiful and filled with golden light
I like to think
That maybe the universe
Was trying to cram in everything for you
Before you died
I can see now
That even the light was telling me
What was coming
Because it looked and felt different
Perhaps it is true what they say
About how the future sends us these hints
To get us ready for the grief

Holding my journal above my head
I read these words about you
Written in the past tense
As if they are raining down on me
And I am drinking them from my JMU cup

When I write about you
I tend to use the present tense
Some find this a bit odd
But I think both tenses are accurate
Since you changed the way I see the world

Maroon and Grey

Maroon and grey always meant number fifty-eight
Maroon and grey always meant happiness
Maroon and grey was always who you were
Maroon and grey was always you
Maroon and grey always made you happy
You spoke of these colors as if they were the epitome of your youth
Maroon and grey represented your success
These colors meant everything to you
Maroon and grey was authentically you

There was never any distance between maroon and grey and you
You became radiant every time these two colors came together
And they reminded you that your glory days were never very far
Marron and grey meant that we brought things to the present
Maroon and grey reflected your greatest passion
Marron and grey was how you manifested elation
Maroon and grey was how you found your way back to your center

Before and After You

Discovering one another
Discovering you
Is akin to the embrace of the sun
Greeting it for the very first time
Before and after you
Places were defined
Simply because I knew you existed
Before and after you
I count the days until we see the sun again
The surrealness of you appears before me
Tossing yourself down on my sofa
Stretching out as if you have always been here
Your darting eyes find my essence
And then you ask after a pregnant pause
To make this memory eternal

I feel proud and I will tell you why
I am proud to wear these colors
My father wanted me to wear his number
To breathe the same success
To feel exhilarated
To teach me who I am meant to be
It embodied strength, character, and drive
I know how important this number was to him
I am keeping the magic of this number alive
I am keeping him relevant
I am proud to be in shape to wear the number properly
I am proud to have reached my goals
I remember when I finished tide pool
He read it in one sitting, moving him to tears
Because I achieved something greater than he had imagined
I am proud to wear this number
Because it has never, ever faded

No More Hands Left to Hold

Desperately
He reaches out
For the one who promised
To be there with him
Until the end
Only to find
There is no hand left to hold
So he holds his own
While wistfully reminiscing
About the good days past
And the ones
He hopes
Are still to come

All-Nighters on Derek's Rooftop

I miss you in times like these
And how we'd sit side by side
On your rooftop garden in SoHo
Huddled under a few layers of afghans
Talking and listening to music all night
Sometimes we read passages from our favorite writers
Other times I read you lines of poetry from my journal
While we sipped on Samuel Adams beer
Until the sun rose over the city
Then we'd watch as its yellow light
Saturated everything on Greene Street
Symbolically burning away the mist of morning
Turning over the world and getting it ready
To begin again

Decay of Love

Since the decay of our love
Quiet whispers of skin-deep guilt
Catch my breath again and again and again

Breathing Through the Chaos

He sits alone on his balcony
Knees against his chest
Breathing in and out
It is here he feels
The sense of the world around him
Its forever shifting currents of air
Their coldness on him
Like a comforting hand

Cowardice of Love

In the cowardice of our love
You didn't heed your own advice

February 17

It has been three years since I was working out on the elliptical when my phone rang. Mike from work was on the other end telling me the horrific news that you died.

It's been three years since I sat on the stairs of the Y for hours, crying and calling our work family telling them the news.

It's been three years since I realized I would never see you again.

It's been three years since I returned to work without you there.

It's been three years since I last looked you in the eye during a conversation.

It's been three years since I first wrote about the evolution of our bond and friendship.

It's been three years since I decided to dedicate my book *kaleidoscope of colors* to you.

Now, three years later, your mural in downtown Somerville is complete and is spectacular.

I've been there often and each time I go I noticed that people have left little notes and cards at the base of the mural.

I love that.

Your legacy continues to affect countless lives.

Your cousin Adrian and I continue to collaborate artistically.

Adrian came by my brand-new condo last year and painted a light blue accent wall in my library.

Light blue was a color you loved, so I know you would love how this looks now and in my condo. Your art hangs in every room, as does Adrian's.

You would love that too.

Your kids are both thriving and continue to follow your example.

Your brother Vincent has realized his dream of becoming a firefighter, citing you as his inspiration.

He continues to do this every day and he saves countless lives.

Your art is displayed all over Somerville, and the bird houses you built and painted still hang in the trees on Bridge Street.

Today I will begin my day by eating one of your favorites, peanut butter and toast.

Today, in the car, on my way to my eye surgery, I will listen to some of your favorite songs and think of you as they play through.

Today I will wear my "Run for Romie" t-shirt underneath my hoodie.

Today, and every day whenever I feel like giving up, I will ask myself, "What would Jerome do?" and then I will keep going.

Holding on Together

Each moment
That is passed back and forth between each other
Alleviates the awful strain
Of having to hold on to time for oneself
Perhaps this is what bonds us together in the first place
The sharing of time
The sharing of the responsibility
Of anchoring oneself in the world
Life is less terrible when you can just rest
For a moment with someone you love
By putting everything down and waiting
Without having to worry about being washed away

The Way I Look at You

New Hampshire is three hours away by train
We won't stay the night
The hotel in Providence is already paid for
The plan is to spend the day
Exploring and then come back

On the train I am hypnotized
By the green fields we pass
Which are laid out neatly in rows
Like the clean lines on the pages
Of the journal resting on my lap
That is still void of any words

I turn away from the window only
When I feel your hand on my ankle
Calling me back
We are facing each other
I have my feet up
On the empty seat beside you
Your fingers are hooked
Underneath the cuff of my jeans
And you're caressing me softly
Not looking up from your book
But I know you're not really reading
Because you are smiling just slightly
With your eyes on the page
Basking in how I look at you

Liar

Liar
Your verities are like small flickers of light
Against the inky black sky
Revealing you are nothing more
Than a plastic smile melting away
On the harsh burn of reality

The First Look of Love

I angle my eyes
Peering up at you with reverence
Your face is warm and flawless
It glows
Making me turn away
Because it feels as if
I am staring directly into the sun

Smile for Me

Once we are back on the train
We eat shrink-wrapped sandwiches
And fig newtons
Sharing the bottle of San Pellegrino
We bought from the little 24-hour bodega
Near the station
Afterwards
We stretch out together on the seats
Settling into a comfortable silence

I see you reach in the pocket of your jeans
And extract a miniature box of Junior Mints
"Would you like some?"
I reach over and take a few from your hand
Allowing my fingertips to play along with yours
Which is both electrifying and thrilling

I see the pleasure you take
In eating these mints
By the way you look at me
Your whole face beams
And I smile too
Because I know this smile of yours
Is for me

Empty Bed

Each night
You consume
Every thought in my mind
Leaving me
To exhale the darkness
In deep sighs
As I fill
The vacant side
Of this queen size bed
With myself

Weekend in Newport, Rhode Island

We step off the train
Heading out towards the center of Newport
Feeling safe in the quiet stillness of the square
We sit on one of the benches there

"I would love to live here, but in a much smaller home, though," I say.
"Obviously with my other half. We'd kiss each other good morning and then
sit at the bay window in our open kitchen and eat eggs on a Sunday
morning. And we would talk."
"What would you talk about?" You ask
"Life, art, books, music."
"Then what?"
"We would walk to the open market and find the perfect food for dinner.
Which we would cook together while the music of Lana Del Rey plays, and
we'd slow dance in the kitchen. Then we'd eat together at the table and talk
more. And we wouldn't let the world intrude upon our life."
You chew on your lip and turn your head to me
A shy smile pulls at the corners of your mouth as you say, "That sounds like
a perfect Sunday, Robert."

Not long after we arrive back at our hotel in Newport, you fall asleep. It is
late and I should be asleep too, but instead I am in the corner huddled
underneath a hotel blanket writing about you in my journal.

I told you earlier that I would want to live in one of the smaller houses here,
but what I really wanted to add and say out loud too was this: "As long as
you are in it."

I want you to know everything about me too. Random things—like my
favorite food is anything I am not supposed to eat and lots of it. And my
favorite thing to do before bed is to read until I fall asleep. And that I sleep
on the left side of the bed, even now that I am single, because I am saving
room and hope. And that I love hot chocolate made with whole milk, but I
don't put any milk on my cereal, unless it is oatmeal. And when I wake up on

Sundays at home and I have no one to share breakfast with or be sweet with, sometimes I feel like crying.

One of the things I love most about you is your ability to know when to not be too serious and the way you navigate our conversations. I like how you squint and consider me for a long time, something that should make me feel self-conscious, but it doesn't. It makes me feel important. Not in the way that causes arrogance or delusions of grandeur. It is the way someone who cares about you makes you feel important, just to them.

I loved this weekend away with you for so many reasons—for its food, jokes, flirtation, and meaningful conversation. I have shared more with you than I have shared with anyone in longer than I can remember; but there is still much more to share, and I cannot wait.

The Fall

Once his heart
Was like a vibrant, overflowing city
With its lights, avenues,
Rooftop gardens in full bloom
But now it is empty
Surrounded only
By boarded-up buildings
And overgrown vacant lots
Filled with nothing
But the dusty decay
Of abandoned dreams

The Train back to New Jersey

We are two people who met by chance
Or sometimes I think we found each other on purpose
And decided to listen to the universe's suggestion

It would have been just as easy for us to decide
There was no point in talking to a stranger
With the expectation that they might be
The very person we needed most that day
But on that day in the library
We both decided to do the opposite
Of what comes naturally to us

I put down my pen and stop writing
Taking in the clickity-clack sound that I love
As this southbound train roars
Through the dead of night

I am sprawled out on the seat next to you
With my journal propped up against my stomach
You turn toward me and link your arm through mine
Before settling back into sleep next to me
Your face pressed against my shoulder

I look at you for a long time
And think about how I could make a whole life
Out of these moments

The Goodbye

The first rays of the sun
Begin to peek over the tops
Of the buildings we pass
The violet-blue of Newark Airport
Slowly turns to gold
"Here comes the sun," I say
You smile and reply, "Oh I love that song!"
So I take out my phone
To find this old Beatles song
In my music library
Then I hit play
Silently we watch the sun climb
Over the tops of the Terminal C
As the song plays, the sun climbs higher
I feel you step into the beam of the sun
That had been warming my face
My whole body is a live wire of nerves
Anticipating this goodbye and dreading it
I feel the warmth of your body move up
Against mine as you bring me into an embrace
I am desperate to know if your eyes are closed like mine
Then I feel you pull back
Bit by bit your fingers loosen
From behind my neck and move down to my chest
For a minute, you let your hand lie there
My eyes are still shut
Afraid to look at you
I feel your hand reluctantly pull away from my chest
Your breath is warm against my face as you say:
"This is only goodbye for now."

Weekend Getaway

It is not the nicest Inn in Princeton
But we like it for its historic view of downtown
Our room is filled with furniture
In varying stages of wear and tear
Its luxury is like a grand gesture abandoned
Even so, we feel a flair of happiness upon entering

You gift me a cheeky smile
Before stepping up onto the bed
Jumping up and down a few times, laughing
I laugh with you
Even as I sense a bit of dread
Just past the edges of what we feel
It is a habit of mine to rush toward an ending
Once I think I can see it
As if the effect of loss is easier to bear this way
I struggle against this, though

When you stop jumping
And stand at the foot of the bed
Throwing your arms out wide
I step toward you
And wrap my arms
Around your waist
Pressing my lips on yours
Even as it creeps back in
The weight of knowing
That this is not right
We are not right
I am still swept away
In the passion of it all
Which only makes me draw you in closer
And kiss you
Harder

The sun is setting in a blue-white sky
As I hop up on the wide rail of my balcony
Dad studies me, smiling in the final brilliance of the day
Before saying, "You look just like Grandpa Cozzi when he was your age."
I smile back, self-conscious
In the haze of dusk
Apparently, this likeness is enhanced
Dad leans against the rail
Looking out at the whispering palmetto trees on the oceanside
We fall uneasily into silence
My eyes meander over the rail
To the sandy grass below
"Rob," Dad says softly
I feel my heart jerk
"Your mother and I have noticed your mood."
Dad's eyes search my face for answers that aren't there
I chew on the inside of my lip nervously
"Do you like Burt?" I ask with a scratch in my throat
I feel the protective happiness
Of Burt's love drape over me as I speak
It rumbles inside of me as I say
"Burt and I are together, Dad. He is my boyfriend."
I reach for the blue sea glass in my pocket
The one Burt gave me on our first date
Rubbing it gently, tracing its curves
I raise my eyes back up to Dad's
I see a familiar warmth I recognize in his eyes
As he says, "Yes, I do like him, and I love you."
"I'm happier now than I have ever been, Dad," I say
Delicately, still a bit self-conscious
But when Dad looks back at me with adoring eyes
I know that nothing has changed between us
We exchange smiles
From around the corner

We can hear Mom talking to Burt
About Pat Conroy's *The Prince of Tides*
Between the rhythm of the waves
Over the sound of the water and wind
We hear the twinkling of wind chimes
Dad nudges me lovingly
As only a father can do
And says, "Let's go talk to your mother and Burt
And fill them in on everything before dinner."

How My Heart Reacts to You

When you speak
My lifeblood sings
And my heart falls a hundred stories
Like a leaf falling from a towering tree
Taken by the wind
Twisting and turning
Until it meets the ground
With a delicate end

The Day I Met Your Mom

Your mother is a petite woman
With dark hair and a warm face
That beams through the screen door
Of her old colonial house
"So, you're Rob," she says
She is wearing a greenish-brown housedress
And younger than I had expected
Perhaps in her early forties
I step into the cool shade of the house
My feet creek and echo
On the hardwood floor of this vintage home
Inside, there are many wonders to behold
So much to be learned from your mom
And from this house with the dark furniture
And antique appointments
In the den there is an easel – I wonder who paints
I need to remember to ask you this question later
There are fresh daisies on the cocktail table
A record player from the 1970's sits atop the bureau
Along with vinyl albums from Puerto Rican artists
Like Hector Lavoe, Jose Feliciano, and Marc Anthony
Above the ancient fireplace
Is a mantel covered with framed photos
I feel a thrill hoping, to see you
As an adolescent, a child, and an infant
The Ricardo I had not been able to know
It is here that I begin to understand
To search for your past in photographs
You were a happy baby, always smiling
Looking right at the camera
As a toddler, I recognize a wide-eyed wonder
Residing within your green eyes,
The very same wonder I see now
The photos of you wearing baseball uniforms

Begin with little league and span all the way to college
Where you played third base as an All-American
No one wears a baseball cap like you, Ricardo
It owns your chiseled, light brown face
Before you, I never found baseball hats sexy
Now I cannot look at one without thinking of you, desiring you
Looking back at this altar of love on the mantel
Allows me to feel what it is like to be an only child
To have your life up to now displayed in its entirety
Your mom smiles at me and says,
"You're all we have been hearing about since Ricardo came home.
Rob says this, Rob says that. Have I told you that Rob writes poetry too?"
"Mom!" a familiar raspy voice shouts
That is when I become aware that you are standing on the stairs
Paused halfway down
Looking luminous in the dimness of the house
Glowing in your Kelly-green three-quarter sleeve
Baseball shirt and white shorts
The matching green and gold cap you wear
Belongs to the beloved high school baseball team you coach
Your curly brown locks seep out
From the front of the cap, covering your eyebrows a bit
Then you look at me and we meet each other's eyes
A smile covers my face at the sight of you
I hope I am not glowing, because I feel like I am
Which only makes me smile more radiantly
"Rob," you say, walking down the stairs and directly to me
You lean in close, so close I can nearly see the pores of your skin
So close your eyes are two worlds
So close I could kiss you right here, in front of your mom
I look down at your hands
Your gold championship baseball ring
Flashes like a beacon in the sun
That streams in through the blinds
We stand there grinning at each other
I fight the compulsion to clasp your hand
Survey it, take note of every line and crease

You study me, squinting in the glare of the day
Like you are considering me, memorizing me
And all I can think about is how
I never want you to look at me any other way

The Rhythm We Have Conceived

We park along the shoreline
Monarch and swallowtail butterflies
Meander erratically above the sea of bluish green
Which presents a glistening palette
Of shifting oranges, blacks, and yellows
Before I can take the key out of the ignition, you're kissing me
Bright, yellow rays trickle in through the sunroof
I grasp one of your hands and place it on my chest, over my heart
As I catch your bottom lip between my teeth
You breathe directly into me, into my moist, hungry mouth
Our passion surges, and I have never felt so alive
This intimacy is potent
We take each other in, with such complete understanding and insight
As we move to this rhythm we have conceived
Afterwards, you lay your head on my chest and we are still
A monarch shutters and trembles over our glowing, gratified bodies
We lay here for so long with the seats reclined that I feel sleep closing in
I kiss the fingers of your hand before moving to the underside of your wrist
Letting my lips linger on this sensitive flesh
Then they move on to the firmness of your stomach
"I can hear your heartbeat," I say to you contentedly,
"It makes me feel strong again."
You respond by softly kissing my neck
Before we drift off together
Into the most peaceful afternoon slumber

Grief in Overdrive

My mother kneels before the French doors
As the sun turns away
Her lavender beach coverup trailing behind her
And for a flash, I think of her, absurdly, as a little girl
She sobs with hard, ripping, breaths
Her head anchored by her hands

She still grieves one year and three months later

I stumble back up the stairs, mouth open, heartbeat racing
Her image is branded behind my eyelids
Guilt and shame rip open every one of my veins

Like a coward, I flee to my room
Where I sit on my bed
Facing the door with terrified eyes
Like I am seeking refuge from a killer
In a low-budget horror film
Blood rushes and roars in my head
I feel weak, pathetic, and unstable
As if someone is tearing up
The hardwood floor below me
Panel by panel
I want to scream
I want to cry
I want to hold my mother gently
But instead, I sit, wondering
What in my life has been real since Dad died
Until I see long, eerie, shadows
Fall across the room
And hear my mother downstairs
Still crying

September 29, 1997

I think about you all the way across the bridge
I think about how helpless you must have felt
I think about your vulnerability
The way you touched my hand before they took you away
I think about how I told myself that you always come back to me
Then the traffic light changes and I cross the street
I have this stupid thought
It should have been raining
When the doctor came in the room
To tell me you were gone
To tell me that you were dead
It should be a different kind of night
It should be starless
It should be bleak
It shouldn't be radiant
I can't quite make myself believe any of it yet
So I imagine the two of us sharing our impressions
On the latest book we have read together
Each one of us sparking the thoughts of the other
I imagine us sitting on your rooftop at dusk, slightly drunk
Going over our thoughts of the day
Talking late into the night
And really understanding something about the world
With the help of New York and literature
Like we are half of each other
Always destined to be friends
We had millions of conversations
That meant something, everything
What else is there anyway?
I swallow what is left of my Coke
Wiping at my eyes
Wondering how I can go on living
When you can't

That Day in Washington Square

On a break from class
I find a spot near the arch in Washington Square
Close to where the acrobats are performing
Passing the hat around for tips

I lose myself in their intricate moves
Feeling the light breeze on my face
I close my eyes and let the world dissolve
Until a feeling on the back of my neck
Causes me to look up
And it's your eyes that catch me
It's always your eyes
My eyes dart down to the pavement below
As I fight the urge to run to you
I bite my lip in surrender
Glancing up hesitantly
Noticing the smallest hint
Of a hopeful smile on your face
You hold out your hand
As if you are offering me a gift
I step toward you and take your hand
You say my name as I say yours
And suddenly, the world contracts

My Rock

Apprehension rises in my gut
As I consider how many lines I've just crossed

Your eyes remain glued to mine
These same browns I've sought comfort from so many times

The flood behind them threatens to spill

I hate seeing you in pain
My rock isn't supposed to crumble

Closing in on the Howl of Loneliness

You meet me on Garfield Street
After my early morning swim in the ocean
You're wearing a light blue tank top
That hangs on your frame
Billowing like a flag under surrender
We walk the side streets
Lined with latent lilac trees
Before making our way
Up to the boardwalk breakfast cafe
Where we take a seat by the water
I am startled but not surprised
When I feel your hand touch mine
It still unsettles me, but not as much as yesterday
"Would you like to go for a walk
And then a swim after breakfast?" I ask
You offer me a vulnerable look
"The truth is, I am afraid of the water."
"That's okay, we can just sit on the beach together then."
I say reassuringly
Ignoring my desire
To ask you more about this fear

After breakfast, we walk
The entire stretch of the boardwalk
Eventually settling on a spot
At the far side of the beach
You prop yourself up on your side
Looking toward the horizon
The silver chain on your chest flashes in the sun
I want to ask you whose ring
Hangs from this chain, but I don't
Beside me are two sea stones
One flat and green,
One white and round

I reach out and pick up the white rock
It is almost transparent
I put it in your hand
And tell you to make a wish
I watch as you close your eyes hard
I pick up the green stone
Holding it in my hand, doing the same
Allowing myself to wish and have a sliver of hope
That maybe you like me as much as I like you
When you open your eyes
I can see that the day's sun has made them sleepy
I bite my lip which tastes salty from my early morning swim
I want to kiss you right here, with the wind in your hair
The essence of the salt air on our clothes
And the tide murmuring beside us
But I refrain
My aloneness roars at the idea
That such a kiss might scare you away
It gnaws hungrily and emptily
Leaving my eyes tearing and my flesh wanting
I say nothing and divert my eyes
To the white stone in your hand
What did you wish for?
I ask myself silently
Wondering if our wishes are parallel
When I look back up, your eyes are droopy
I watch as you slowly doze off
Your sunglasses are on the ground between us
I am propped up on my side
Letting my eyes wander down the length of your body
To your abdomen, which is slightly covered with sand
To your legs with the same walnut-colored hair
That flops in your eyes
I have the most uncontrollable urge
To place the palm of my hand
On the smoothness of your stomach
But I cannot, at least not yet

I content myself with a lingering look
Before taking your sunglasses in my hand
So they won't be crushed in our sleep
I turn onto my back, lying still
Trying to control my breathing
As I, too, drift off to sleep

A Few Lifetimes

I really don't want to be here
As Julie speaks, her voice recedes
Until it sounds like she is whispering
From a cave at the other end of the world
I know she is lying about the new guy
On your volleyball team having eyes for you
Yet I have never known such raging jealousy
I haven't adapted to loving you yet
Let alone to the idea that I might someday lose you
I cannot bear losing anyone else
I walk away from her and head to the kitchen
Where you are playing that spoons card game
You regard me through buzzed, blue-hooded eyes
Your smile is so genuine, and it tells me
You are having a good time with your teammates
This simple gesture releases a portion of my despair
But I still must get out of here for a little while
Once outside, I go to my car
I sit on the hood and look obtusely out to the sea
Wanting so much to succumb to my sadness
Because fighting it is like trying to resist anesthesia
I can no longer remember a time in Charleston before Derek
Suddenly, I hear something from the house
You are standing inside the screen door
 Holding our windbreakers
You appear angelic with the light behind you
The image makes my heart throb
You flick the light off, letting the screen door slam behind you
Heading over to join me on the hood of the car
I don't say anything
You place a hand on the back of my neck
And say, "I didn't realize that you were so sad."
I offer you a pained smile before uttering, "I didn't either."
"I miss him too, Rob."

You lean back and pull me back with you
So that we face the panorama of stars above
They sparkle and glimmer like a promise
I hear you make a sound of contentment
The moon reflects in the wetness of your mouth
On your golden blond hair
In your eyes of azure
While you look at the stars and I look at your cheek
I can see the curve of your lashes
The scruff of your five o'clock shadow that has begun to surface
The arch of your throat when you swallow your beer
Then you turn and our noses almost touch
The energy between us is charged
Your lips are parted and shiny from your drink
My breaths are uneven and quick before we kiss
I know that this is just a fleeting, intimate moment
But to me, it feels like a few lifetimes

October 4, 1997

Since I am unable to sleep
I decide to take the thirty-five-minute ride
To the Jersey Shore
I get to the beach quickly
Because there is almost no one
On the road this late at night
Being at the ocean quells my nerves
The sound of the waves reminds me of you
The night is all salt air and smell
It's all memory too
Of summer, swimming, night walks
Hunts for sand dollars and sea glass
Towards the lighthouse, there is the spot
Where we sat and talked
During our last trip here fourteen days ago
I close my eyes and see us
Huddled there in our NYU hoodies
Hanging on to the last days of September
I open my eyes and scan
The entirety of the beach
Looking for a sign of your presence
Or perhaps you are here already
As one of the people I see
Walking the shoreline tonight
Because I believe in ghosts and past lives
Just as you did
You loved to read about them

Every time I stand on the beach now
I wish us back to nine days before you died
Or to any day before you died
With what I know now
Maybe I could save you
I walk up to a quiet spot

At the end of the beach
I dig myself into the cool October sand
Burying my legs past my hips, I stare at the water
It's glistening with moon silver all over the surface
I have tried to stop thinking
About the day you died, Derek, but I can't
I hear your last words, "I'll be back."
I hear the squeaky wheels of the stretcher
Rolling you away
But I also hear your bare footsteps on the sand
I see you diving into on oncoming wave
Your long, slender arc disappearing into the sea
And all I can think about
Is how 1997 had been a good year
For both of us
And how the universe
Cheated you

Lost Boys Among the Legends

Derek is as happy as I am
When we leave the Roxy at five in the morning
We are tired, a little buzzed, both sore from falling on the roller rink
I probably shouldn't have tried to teach Derek how to skate backwards
Thank goodness for the six foot five Diana Ross drag queen who helped us
up when we tumbled to the floor under the blinding strobe lights
She was an expert skater dressed in leather and lace
Wearing all of Miss Ross's mannerisms
We launched into a giggle fit after she called us "Lost boys among legends"
For skating on the inside track
With the featured skaters
Clearly, we didn't know any better
I laugh again now, and Derek just looks at me
And asks through his own laugh, "Miss Ross?"
He puts an arm around my shoulder, nudging me a bit too hard
We nearly lose our footing again, which only makes us laugh more
There isn't a single other person on W 18th Street as we walk
But the way it is lit, warmly, dripping orange and yellow
It is almost as if it is extending an invitation to us
I feel more alive than ever this morning
There is something tugging at my chest
As I walk alongside Derek, all I can think about
Is this first night at this iconic nightclub
Because, as strangely as this sounds, it feels like I have been accepted
Into a special, secret New York City society
One that had been out of reach for me
Before Derek

Disappearing into You

We step outside
As David Bowie's "Let's Dance"
Blares through the speakers
Drowning out the sounds of the city
It is raining lightly, and we huddle
Under the entrance of Rebecca's apartment building
You prop an elbow against the arched wooden door
I watch you run your hand through your perfect messy hair
The overhead light illuminates you like in an Italian museum exhibit
To these eyes, you are the New York version of the statue of David
You take out a lighter and flick it
No fewer than a dozen times before it catches a flame
You light your joint and shoot me a look
That should scare me more than it does
The idea of a tryst with no permanence
Is a new approach for me but I have a desire
That needs to be satiated
I am drunk, my eyes are slightly out of focus
But I can see that desire lives in your shadow light
It penetrates the corner of my consciousness
Spilling onto the pavement where you stand
The silence hangs between us
As you skillfully level me with your eyes
Your touch eases onto my flesh
It is surprisingly soft and balanced
Rippling like waves in my veins
As I disappear into you

You

There are many thoughts
Running through my head
After I leave New York
But I can only focus on one
You

Were you flirting with me?
I know it sounds impossible
Someone like you
Engaging, confident
And so comfortable in their own body
Could not be further out of my league

I try to push your face out of my head

It doesn't work

Because my mind immediately travels back
To the clean, smooth lines of your body
The strap of your loose tank top
Drifting to the edge of your shoulder
Your greenish-brown eyes
And the full lips that curl up at one corner
As if you have a secret you want to tell me

I force myself to shift my mind away from you
So I don't miss my stop on the train

Looming Threat

I want to hold on to you
As long as I can
But I know it is not possible

When you reach out to hold my hands
Your eyes are welling
No tears yet
But the formation of them
Like a looming threat

Your eyes are fuller now
A wave is coming to the surface of your face
About to burst

The words of rejection
I have been expecting
Come out slowly
With a benevolence
That only enrages me

Mirrored Shadows

Even in the dark
His world is still uneven
Jagged
Psychedelic
Like bits of glass
Fitting erratically together
In a shadowy hall of mirrors

More than Friends?

Counting Crows are playing on the radio
As we pull out of the city
I look over at you for a second
You are a hybrid now
The old you with the sinking broken heart
And the new you with a buoyant heart
With possibly some future you
Tucked under your skin
The day pours in
When you roll down the window
Sunshine and morning dust fill the car
Once we reach the outskirts of the city
The concrete drops away
The trees
And sky get bigger
Stretched in pale blue
The road vibrates softly
Through the window
Humming you to sleep
When you awake
We are in Cape May Point
You look around, smiling
Smelling the loose salt air of the ocean
I watch as you wrap your arms around yourself
Following me onto the boardwalk
We are standing so remarkably close
That the friendly conversation feels sexy
I look straight into your eyes
Searching for a hint
That there is something more
Between us than friendship
And I think I see it in your face

Riptide

His anxiety forms quickly
Eating away at his confidence
Like a riptide through a weak coastline
He is the sand tumbling in the raging water

More than Friends? II

I can hear the water
As we move closer
The hush of it
Circling and leveling out
When it appears, I sigh
It is low tide and achingly flat
Not like the waves
That heap over themselves continually
At high tide
You and I sit on the beach
And stare at the water for a long time
I watch the ocean and you
You make a sandcastle
With a carefully placed ring of shells
Around the walls
It is a bit lopsided
But I appreciate
The artistic expression

Before we leave to check in
To our bed-and-breakfast
You walk to the edge to wash your hands
I think you do this deliberately, though
Because when you return
You splash me
I can feel the water on my skin
As I laugh and retreat

There is a soft pink glow in the sky
That reflects on the water now
Making it look like a pink mirror in a blue frame
And when you call from up ahead
You say my name in a way no one ever has
You say it in the same way you say love
That must mean something, right?

Disappeared but Not Gone

We are a few miles out to sea
The wind is gusty
But the sky is clear
Up above, the American flag flaps noisily
As its flagpole clanks
The sound reminds me
Of the Shore Acres house my grandparents owned
Every day, my grandfather would raise the flag proudly
I loved helping him and to this day
The sound of a flag blowing in the breeze
Is soothing

I am thankful for this blustery day

Standing on the deck while looking back at St. Simons Island,
Which, along with New York City,
Was your favorite place in the whole world
I consider the possibility of a soul moving on after death
The moment when your ashes were scattered
In the aquamarine-colored water
When I realized you were gone for good
That moment would have been much easier
If I had known
That the center of you
The thing that made you *you*
Had traveled somewhere
Disappeared but not gone
Turning into something else
Even turning into the puffy white clouds
Would have been better than ash

The Warmth of Your Hand Leaving Mine

You hold my hand
Tapping your thumb against mine
Keeping beat to "Rhiannon"
The song playing from my Sony Walkman
Into the headphones we share

This memory
Of our final moment together
Is the only good thing
About the day you died

At the start of every September
It is impossible not to think about this day

Today I think a lot about
How I could have gotten through
Quite a bit in this life
With you holding my hand
But I do know this for certain:
When I grow older
And memories fade like the wind
I will still be able to feel the warmth
Of your hand leaving mine

Option B

I study every inch
Of the pattern on the placemat
Concentrating on the blue and yellow triangles
I trace them with my eyes
Finding the end one
And following it around to the start of another
It is the same placemat that has always been here
Every table in the diner has one
But I have never noticed the triangles before
I guess this makes sense
How I stare down at them now
Considering I no longer have the desire
To meet the eyes of the one
Who has just made it clear to me
That I am nothing more
Than their option B

Dear Derek (4/16/2021)

All my insecurities are circling me today. Insecurities about who I have become and how my new limitations are affecting my most important relationships. I am someone different now and sometimes, most of the time, this is a difficult truth to face. I often forget how much permanent change has invaded my world. Is this me living in denial and running from reality? I worry that these physical limitations will cause people to leave. People I cannot imagine being gone from the center of my life. I don't want to be replaced, Derek. I don't want them to find someone else's center because I need them in my center. Am I overreacting? Perhaps so, but this fear is so real that it breaks my skin.

Every single day I mourn the loss of the things I can no longer do, but then I hear your voice in my head reminding me that not everything is lost completely. I just need to do them differently and carefully. My mind is a mess today, can you tell?

In an effort to pull myself out of the muck, I have moved to the library room where I sit by the open window and breathe in the scent of the spring rain. I reach for a book from my book cubes. I grab your Eliot Ness book. I was with you when you bought this used, second edition. I remember us both being amazed that it was in such good condition for an old book. Immediately, I turn to the photos located in the middle. The faces of Capone and Ness are hypnotic. They glow from the pages in brilliant, clear black and white. I sit on the floor examining every photo. I stop at the picture of Eliot in his field uniform. There is a tiny arrow pointing to the picture and three words next to it, written in small, loopy letters, the kind of letters you used: "An absolute boss." Without a doubt, it is your handwriting. I know from the way the tail of the *s* kicks upward. I know it because you loved Eliot Ness. I know because you loved this picture. I know it in a way I can't prove. This doesn't make me sad exactly. It's a feeling I can't seem to name. I think about it for several minutes. I decide the feeling has something to do with you writing in this book along with other people who no longer exist in this world. The traces of them are hidden inside lines and letters etched in ink in a book from which no one can borrow.

Today, the notes I write in my own margins contain my biggest worries. I don't want to be discarded or exchanged for something newer or better. All of this worrying has no practical use, Derek. I know this is exactly what you would say right now but I am already deep in the blue that hit me earlier and I don't know how to climb out.

-R

The Last Trip to St. Simons

A breeze flutters the white gossamer curtains
Out to the balcony where I stand
Bringing with it
The soft scent of freshly cut grass
The sibilance of the ocean
And the whisper of the willow's branches

Inside,
Your bedroom is precisely how I remember it
Your king-size bed
Is against the south wall
Parallel to the sea
My eyes stop at the bookcase
Remembering how we would
Read aloud to one another
Pausing at the passages we wished to discuss
Atop the bookcase sits a framed picture of you
In your prep school uniform
Taken when you were about fifteen
Even then you had been beautiful
Far more beautiful than the other boys in the picture

I huddle under the soft blue and white afghan on your loveseat
Trying to write something about you
Over on your dresser
I spot your watch
The one you bought in Little Italy
On the first day of the Feast of San Gennaro
I hold it up to the light
Its face is stopped permanently at 11:11
I guess watch batteries don't last a year after all
I bite down on the sleeve of my hoodie
Thinking about the last time I saw you smile
The soft rasp of your morning voice

And how your hand felt in mine
On the last day you were alive
Has it really been a year?

Later today
This house of yours
Will leave me forever too

Keeping You from the Void

When I answer the phone
Your voice has the sad tone I recognize

You must have lost a patient today

Once we hang up
I make your favorite comfort food
Sloppy Joes on potato rolls
With macaroni and cheese and broccoli

We eat in the living room
Talking little
Afterward, we lie on the sofa
Neither one of us gets up to turn on a lamp
The only light we have
Comes from the flickering images of the television
Dancing over our faces like taunts

The hiss of static from the television
Sounds like the high whisper of ghosts
The light of those images pulls and claws
At our slumbering forms
We lie together
Facing the television
My arms around yours
Protecting you from falling into the void

Ode to Sal Mineo

I was younger than 14. I do not remember the age when I first watched you on a TV screen. I was fidgeting because I found you magnetic and attractive and I didn't know what that meant. The magnetic pull you had over me was different than the way I felt about James Dean and his charisma. You were the one I could not take my eyes off as I watched your rebellion unfold. I saw a little of myself in you because, to the observant eye, I was a bit of an outsider too, although my situation was not as obvious or as intense as yours. To be an outcast means that you are never able to completely show yourself, but when you meet James and Natalie, I feel happy for you because you slowly begin to reveal yourself to them. Seeing your friendship with James and Natalie unfold, gave me insight into how quickly true friendship can develop.

Because of you, I am reminded of when I met Chuck. He and I recognized each other's emptiness and we understood how to fill that void for one another. Watching you on the TV screen I was hypnotized and mesmerized by the thought of you. I remember being confused by this reaction to you. Before that night, I had some in person experience with nice looking boys who made me feel uneasy and jittery, but this reaction to you was different. It was a fascination that transcended a mere physical attraction. It was much bigger than that and Dad noticed how fixated I was to the screen. The emotions traveled all through my body and my eyes followed your every movement. I thought a lot about how much I wanted to be your friend, to be part of this trio of you, James, and Natalie.

To explore the landscape of our youth and plan the adventures we all craved. I imagined us riding in a convertible, singing out loud to the songs on the radio as we drove along the coast. I wanted to hold your hand and make you feel safe and secure. I wanted you to feel comfortable enough to lay your head across my lap and fall asleep while I gently brushed the hair from your forehead. When I looked at you, I saw love, a new kind of love that I have never experienced before with someone close to my age. Every thought I had become a possibility. You were vulnerable but you were the rebel who pushed back. You accepted love freely because you longed for this honest kind of love all your life. James and Natalie provided this for you, but I wanted to give you my love too.

Maybe this was just the imaginative mind of my younger self, but I swear I could see it. When Dad gave me a cup of hot chocolate, it warmed my hands as I watched your storyline reach a climax. My tears came as a surprise when I saw them fall into the piping hot chocolate. I didn't want this ending for you. The pain on James's face became my pain too. I could almost feel the bullets in the palm of my hand when James yelled back at the police officers, "I have the bullets, I have the bullets!" Dad pulled me into a hug that lasted through the ending credits. He asked if I was okay. I told him I wasn't expecting you to die. I wanted to see you again as this character. I remember Dad telling me that many times the special ones are taken from us too soon but since they are special, our memory of them never fades. I went to sleep that night thinking about you and recalling everything about you. Every gesture, every facial expression, the tone of your voice, the sound of your tears. As I waited for *Rebel Without a Cause* to be shown on television again, you resided inside my dreams.

Aunt Nettie had a framed photo of you in her house. I loved looking at each time I visited. She had bought it at some boardwalk photo stand back in the late 1950's. Now, this photo of you resides in my home library. I love looking at your beautifully sculpted face that imbues softness, sensitivity, and strength.

The picture I have of you in my bedroom tells the perfect story because it's everything I imagine it to be. You on a boat sunbathing on the water with a book in your hand was the beginning of how I saw love. I own the film now and every so often I watch, and each time I become that boy again, fascinated by you and a little bit in love with you.

258

Our Last Week Together

The beach is crowded when we arrive at dusk
The scents of beer and burgers carry over the sea of people
You and I make our way through the multitude
Stepping over feet and drinks
And touching the edges of quilted blankets
A young girl runs by with a sparkler
Her cheeks puffed in excitement
From the boardwalk pavilion
We hear the band playing Tom Petty's "American Girl"

The first firework explodes
Just as we set our blanket down on the sand
The crowd oohs collectively
I look over to see your face lit up
With red, white, and blue confetti
You smile at me, placing your hand
On the blanket so our little fingers touch
Fireworks scream and glitter overhead
Neon oranges, golds, and reds paint the blackness
Silvers, violets, and blues flash and shimmer
Silent sparks rocket into the dome of black sky above
Exploding into brilliant flowers
Of whistling pinks, greens, and whites
Attacking the dark with booms and cracks
Wavering above us like charged specters
The children next to us chase fireflies
And write their names in the air with sparklers
Like shooting stars captured for their fleeting felicity

The sky glimmers and dances
Glowing in ephemeral sequins
Lighting the eyes and visages of onlookers

When it is over

The night seems darker than before
As the consequential smoke
Begins drifting over us
Unabashedly foreshadowing
The regret
We would soon feel

American Hourglass

In this American hourglass
Filled with tears
Each drop falls violently
With the force of a ballistic missile

Another Missed Opportunity with You

I lean over
Throwing you a wide high five
After we beat Nick and Kristen at Pictionary
When our hands meet
Our fingers slide together
Connecting

The mood in the room changes

Looking down into your perfect face
Our hands are frozen together
And I feel almost trapped
Unsure of what will happen next
I want to pull you up out of the chair
And kiss you in front of everyone
But I am also afraid of the exact same thing
The panic must show on my face
Because you slide your hand away from mine gently
Leaving me to lament over
Another missed opportunity with you

The Cold Family Estate

My anxiety hums
As I walk inside alone
Nobody is even glancing at me
But I cannot shake the feeling
That they are all watching me
From the corners of their eyes
Judging me

Outside
The dark shadows celebrate the rain
Inside
I walk in echo of our footsteps
Feeling the same cold marble floor
Under my feet
That we felt
When we walked in here together
For the first time

Back then
I remember being struck by
How this childhood home of yours
Which was so luxurious and grand
Could feel so unbelievably cold inside
Devoid of any traces of love

Tonight
It feels even colder

That June Day on the Beach with You

Grief seems to find me
When I least expect it to
Like on this day on June
During a trip to the ocean with you

After a long swim
I fall onto my back beside you on the blanket
You turn toward me
Lifting yourself up on your side
"Hey," you say
Your voice solicitous
I put my hand over my face
Which is wet with salt water and tears
I am embarrassed
When you ask, "What's wrong?"
I do not answer
But you pull my hand away
Which makes me cry harder somehow
Then you kiss me on my forehead
And then both cheeks and my lips
When I try to pull away
You grab my head with both your hands
Holding me in place
While making your funniest faces
Speaking in your overexaggerated Spanish accent
Until I am laughing instead of crying
You laugh too, rolling on top of me
Gently laying your head on my chest
Where we stay
Breathing in unison
Until we drift off into a midday nap

Covert Gestures

I remember falling asleep
To Ray LaMontagne's "Lesson Learned" last night
His voice light-bodied and pure
Embodying my every ambition
As I listened, I thought about
The lessons you and I have learned
How we got here
To our "agreed" separation

I feel a tinge of hope
Sitting beside you now

On the brick wall in front of us
We watch James Dean and Sal Mineo
In *Rebel Without a Cause*
Their images standing out more eerily
From Rebecca's old film projector
And it is so painful not to touch you
Even to reach my hand to yours
Would be a mistake
Caution is an instinct of ours now
But we still have our repertoire of covert gestures
The brushed elbow or knee
The slight pressure of a foot
And we make use of them
As the night deepens and the air chills

Current State

He has worn himself down
To a bearable size
Through an erosion
Necessary to survive

Tempting Fate by Being So Happy

When I see you the next day
I am not sure what to feel or how I am supposed to act
What if you look at me in broad daylight and want to run?
But when I kissed you last night, you kissed back
We face each other on opposite sides of the kitchen
With lips swollen from kissing
And eyes puffy from lack of sleep
Both a little unsure

When we get to the ocean, we sit for a time
In silence after I turn off the car
We don't look at each other
Eventually, we get out and go down to the sand
I settle into my beach chair
Watching you stray into the shallow water
You look like art with your soccer player legs
Tight waist and flat chest
I wonder if I'll ever be able to touch your body again
You turn to face me and don't see the swell coming
It crashes into you, thrusting you forward
You laugh with a child's abandon at the surprise of it
Striving to maintain balance against the force of the surf
A few minutes later, you trek back up to join me
I am glad you choose not to speak
Because I am not sure what is appropriate
I want to know if you are okay with what happened last night
But instead, I sit quietly, trying not to breathe too loudly
I gaze at you, leaning back in your white swimsuit, facing the sea
The simplicity of your face steals my breath
We kiss
It is different in the light of day
Being able to see makes it so much more real
We lay on the beach for hours, kissing
Because it is so new

Kissing until our lips are sore
I am surrounded by your body, your ardor
Your heat, your firmness, and your mouth
Your long black hair blows in the wind
I push it back out of your face
Reveling in the freedom I feel

Later that night, we get pizza and head back to your beach house
Birds chatter nervously in the moist, heavy dark
In anticipation of the oncoming storm
The white noise of wind rushes loudly through the trees
A flash of lightning, like a jagged violin bow sizzles across the sky
The world around us lights up like a photoflash
Before we are cast in pitch black again
Our eyes tormented by the specters of light
A furious overture of cicadas plays around us

Once inside the house, we set our things down in darkness
Because the electricity is out
When you turn to speak, lightning lights up your face
Or maybe your face lights up the room, I can't tell
Words fail me
I lead you onto the screened-in front porch
Air sings through the screens
Rattling the wind chimes, creaking the swing, ruffling our hair
We sit on the swing and eat our pizza, watching the storm
After we finish, we sit in silence, huddled up against one another
I stroke your hair and smile when your breathing changes
You have fallen asleep with your head under my chin
And in this moment, I understand what you meant
By fearing you would tempt fate by being so happy

The Final Out of Our Love

I obsess
Over our diminishing love
Until one night
In our bed
My skin clammy in the tepid breeze
Crickets ring in the dark
I know what to do
I need to tell you everything
Perhaps my admission will prompt yours
Then we can deal with our pain together
We need to get back the peace
We have known for so many years
The same peace I have based my beliefs on
I need to know there had been tranquility
Living inside our love once
But what if it had never been?
What if I had imagined it all?
What then?

Lying flat on my back
I put my arm across my eyes
And see you next to me
With your hand brushing mine
It's this small point of contact
That I focus on

As I drift off to sleep
The world softens and recedes
Until it feels like I am floating
On a sea made of soft leaves
That guides me back home

December 5, 2018

When you hold out the bag with the rest
Of the Baked by Melissa peanut butter cupcake
My fingers brush against yours and there is a feeling
Like a firecracker in my stomach
And then, something shifts

For my entire life
I have looked for signs
Like in poetry and verse
Like in everything
I have waited for things to feel just right
To feel like the universe
Had finally given me its blessing

Perhaps you never really get that, though
Because the world tends to tell you
Repeatedly
In as many ways as it knows how
That you are not good enough
So you must fight for your place in it
No matter what,
No matter who you are

If you're lucky, what you share
With someone can reshape
The way the world spins around you
So whatever this shifting feeling is
I am all in

The Final Goodbye?

When you thank me
For returning your keys
I nod my head
Before making a move
Toward the door
Your full lips
Slip into a small grin
As you stand beside me
With your hand resting
On the back of your neck
When I turn the doorknob
I hear my name
So I turn to face you again
My heart makes its way
Up to my throat
If you ask me to stay
I am not sure
I can convince myself
To say no

The Last New Year's Eve with Derek

We sit on the living room floor
With our backs up against the couch
In front of the fireplace
Both of us are a little tipsy
From drinking on near-empty stomachs
As I raise my glass to yours
The firelight dances through it
I watch it undulate
Writhing in the liquid
Golden bubbles ripple
Up the champagne's surface
"To eternal friendship," we both say quietly
And then louder in unison
Imbuing the words
With all our desire for the future
Up on the roof
A chorus of voices can be heard
Ringing through the New York night
Singing "Auld Lang Syne"
At the top of their lungs
I glance at the fire burning
It is a blue blur, like a stormy eye
But crackling and warm
The celebration continues upstairs without us
I watch as you drift off
Your kelly-green New Year's hat on the floor between us
Your face is tranquil
And your skin is smooth, olive and unmarred
I pick up your hat and put it on my head
Thinking about everything we have planned
To do together in the new year
It gives me a warm, solid feeling
Then I, too, drift cozily into the slumber
Of the new year

Terrifying

I can hear the ocean
Coming through the window
Its vibration accompanies the incoming breeze
Your blond curls blow softly under my chin
As you lie face up across my chest
Your eyes are glowing like sparkling sapphires
Against the muted light of the room
When you tell me that you love me for the first time

It catches me by surprise
Leaving me elated and terrified
A feeling
That reminds me
Of something my grandfather said
After he saw the ocean for the first time
He said it was the most beautiful thing he had ever seen
And the thing that terrified him the most
I look back at you and say, "I love you too," with smiling eyes
And I think
Perhaps all things that are worthwhile
Are terrifying

Date with Another Poet

The sun is shooting reds, oranges and greens
Across the water
The scent of lavender merges
With the savory sea air
I lean on the railing and inhale deeply
So nervous that my teeth are chattering
Then I hear my name
I go to the stairs to find you
Standing on the sand
Poetry books in hand
You are a vision in white linen shorts
And an aqua sweatshirt
Your hair, just beginning to curl under
Twists in the wind
"Hi," I breathe
Not knowing if the word
Is lost in the wind
"Hey," you say
Your eyes the size of the sun
I attempt to say something
Clever and sophisticated
But as I descend the stairs
All I can do is stare

Dear Derek (12/2/1997)

As I drive out of the Holland Tunnel on this Tuesday afternoon in my '92 Acura Integra, it doesn't seem all that long ago that I was sucking in my breath while teaching you how to drive a stick shift. You loved this car, and I remember the look on your face when you shifted into fifth gear for the first time. We laughed when you drove through the tunnel because we both had the exact same image at the same time, the image of Lucy Ricardo making a U-turn in the Holland Tunnel and backing up traffic from the city to East Orange, New Jersey. A smile covers my face at the thought of that day, and for a minute, it makes me forget everything else. In my last grief counseling session, Scott asked me to imagine how I'd feel leaving the city behind for a while. "Light," I told him, explaining that I would be relieved because I wouldn't have to run into any of our friends I have drifted away from since your death. I wouldn't have to see people from the Greene Street Bookstore, or the kids I read to there every other week.

I don't feel light or relieved today, though. For one thing, I haven't driven into the city since you died, and the traffic has been so heavy that I have yet to shift into fifth gear. And then there is this box of yours that your sister put in the trunk before I left your loft for the last time. I hate that your life ended as a set of boxes with things written on them like "Photos," "Sports Stuff," "Books," "CDs," and "Notebooks." Sarah packed them all. The box in my trunk is full of items Sarah couldn't categorize, so she wants me to go through it because she believes that many of these items are tied to me and you. There is a question mark written in black Sharpie on the side of the box and the words "Miscellaneous Derek/Rob stuff" under that. I have this feeling that I'll be driving around with it in my trunk for as long as I have this car.

I nearly pull over at the thought and hurl it from the guardrail. One good throw and it would be gone for good. Everything is working against me, though, the pale blue color of the sky, the sunlight, and your scolding tone that I hear ringing in my ears. It's the exact time of day that you and I drove in this car for the last time. We looked for Giants Stadium as we approached New Jersey, the way we always did, spotting it first in small circular curves and then in deep scoops.

Once we passed the stadium, the highway opened, and we drove fast. The music was always loud and fast and usually Stevie or Springsteen. We'd sing at the top if our lungs, while keeping beat on the dash and the steering wheel. Now, as I reach this same stretch of highway, I push the car as fast as it will go. The marsh lands outside and beyond the stadium move backward in a blur, and I imagine time rewinding, back to when the world was a different place. I keep driving fast, looking through the rearview mirror, waiting for the asphalt to rise and the city's skyline to disappear.

-R

The Lie I Crave

The wind chimes ring
Louder and louder from the porch
As we stand exchanging worried looks
I loosely interpret as an irritated sigh
"You love him?" I ask again
"Yes," you say
"I love him, sorry."
I search your eyes for the lie I crave
But all I see there is the truth
The sobering realization
That to you
I no longer matter

I Want it Back

I wish I could tell you the story
Of how you caught my eye
And how I wanted that look
I gave you back

Leveling the Chaos

They are blue like a cloudless day
With flecks of darker sapphire
I study them
Letting them burn into my mind
Memorizing their intricate patterns
Comparing each
Noting parallels and differences

These eyes
I need them
To level the chaos inside

The Air of Unwelcomed Solitude

Silence enters the room from all sides
In intersecting patterns
You see soft pinks and whites
Floating above
Sounds screech from outside
Car horns
A cat's purr
And some noises you can't quite recognize
When you close your eyes
You hear yourself humming
And then the harrowing silence sets in
Along with the air of unwelcomed solitude
And a heartbeat that will never die
Can be heard behind the veil of everything

Incapable of True Love

True love
Isn't just about looking someone in the eyes
It is also about looking with them

Facing what they face

I wonder
If there is anyone you can stand with and watch
What you wouldn't watch with me

The First View of Love

Hope is the color of gold
She shines brightly like the only star
That matters in the sky
She is bound to me
In her essence for all eternity
She is the ocean of every smile I will ever see
The universal creed
That will envelop me for all my days
Devotion is a word I do not have to define
She is timeless
She is my paradise
She is my favorite song
The one that I always sway to
She is my perfect view
The equivalence
To the first view of love
Does not exist

Resentment

His written words are trapped
In between shallow breaths
Held prisoner
By an aching lump of hostility
In the back of his throat

Our Words Will Outlive Us

Together we carved poetic words
Deep into the tree trunk
Because we wanted
The passion held by our words
To outlive us

Separation

As I walk slowly onto the back porch
Toward the stained-glass table set for two
My eyes fixate on the swaying trees

The sun has just set
And maybe it is the pending distance
That is about to be put between us
But the towering tree limbs
Normally so beautiful
Seem ominous and foreboding
As if the shadowy branches
Can read my mood

Centering

The beach is quiet
The gulls have all returned to their nests
He has the edge of the inlet to himself
Except for a few other anonymous watchers nearby
He glances at them briefly
Wondering what shape their lives hold
If they are content
Or if they have come down here
Looking for tranquility too
He hugs his knees and puts his chin
On his arms, closing his eyes
Allowing the soothing sound of the ocean
Spilling into the inlet to sink in
The water below him splashes up a little
Spraying the edges of his shorts
If only the ocean could wash his memory clean
So he could forget all about earlier
When he spoke three words
That were never returned

The Gift

The gift of insanity awaiting me in dreams
Is your voice etched in whispers
That cuts through
The inky darkness
In illumination
As it takes flight
Surrounding me
In colors of lust
That are impossible to resist

Our Next to Last Day Together

I awake at ten
The overcast morning
Is shockingly bright and cool
The smothering heat of the previous day gone
You are standing at the screen door
Chewing at your cheek
There are small dark pouches
Under your eyes
An intimation of unease
In the set of your mouth
The sterling sky and the aqua sea
Battle for precedence behind you

When you walk back over to the bed
The brown of your skin is a sharp contrast
To the ocean of sheets
You offer me a bittersweet smile
The sweet wins out, though
Because I know you are happy I am awake
We hang there for a few quiet seconds
Enjoying this unspoken connection

You climb back in bed
Settling into me
Resting your chin on my shoulder
Your breath is hot on my ear

In this moment
We are more ourselves
No pretenses
No feelings of impending doom
For this rebound relationship
Instead
It is a moment of clarity

We are experiencing
A quiet moment
That lulls us both back to sleep

Fade to Black

The ice that forms on the window
Cracks in spiderweb veins
That look just like shattered mirrors
Outside
The sky is flat and starless
As though the world
Has suddenly become a sealed box

Ever since you died
I have been unable to sleep
I sit by the French doors
In the big green and white armchair
The one with the matching ottoman
That you bought specifically
For reading and stargazing

I stare up at the sky for a long time
Knowing that behind the blackness
Are planets and stars and galaxies
But I don't believe in them anymore

Sandcastle for Two

Once you reach the jetty
I hold out my hand to you
Helping you get steady footing
So you can join me in looking out at the sea

The sun is hot on our heads and blinding on the water
We look at the horizon for a few moments
Then you say, without turning from the view
"You're the first person who has made me feel
Like I am not different and weird."
I say, "Maybe that's because you're not so different."
You don't utter a word in response
Choosing instead to awkwardly sing
The opening bars of "Moon River"
Rendering it clear to me that this is your attempt
To segue into something else. Anything else
My heart gasps, "What made you sing that?"
"It is the last song I played on the piano this morning."
The iconic song reminds me of Derek and Diana
Slow dancing one twilight summer ten years ago

I sit in silence so long
Lost in this memory of my late friend and his fiancée
That I become aware you are staring at me
Your eyes squinched in the sun
"I just miss him," I offer
"Especially in summer and especially here."
You look at me carefully for a minute
As if planning some sort of a distraction
"You know what I want to do?" You ask excitedly
Rubbing your hands together
"Make a sandcastle! Come on, Rob!" You say
Pulling me up on my feet

We build one
You sculp
While I fetch water
It turns out lumpy and crumbly
But we are both happy
"It doesn't matter how it looks," you say
"It's ours!"

Parked

Inside your car
Parked along the boardwalk
We create a haven just for us
Listening to the heavy drumming of rain
On the roof of your Toyota
As we watch white caps
Atop the ocean waves
Roll in and out
Clawing at sand and shells
Tossing pieces of driftwood
Across the shore

I lean over to rest my head
Against your shoulder
Absentmindedly staring down
Along the curve of your arm
Toward your long piano fingers

We sit in this comfortable silence
Until the delicate saltwater scents
And the sensual summer heat
Trigger our intimacy

Desirous eyes
Hold our gaze
As fingertips gently slide over frames
Whimsical touch spills our wildest desires
Before the map charting our course
Leads us to a gratifying
Crescendo

The Slow-Motion Movie Montage

Summer has arrived with its steamy, sultry days
I watch you from my front porch
As you make your way across the lawn
The rain is pouring in the sunshine
I want to ask you how long it has been
But I have it down to the day
 I stop, and we look at each other and laugh
I run to you
Lifting you up off the ground
As we fall into a warm embrace
I close my eyes and spin you around in my arms
Seeing in textbook clarity
Our technicolor world resurrecting
In a kind of slow-motion movie montage
Where every thought is possibility
Ballooning around us

When I open my eyes, though
I only see the pale white color
Of my bedroom ceiling
Staring back

The Beginning of the End

"We love each other, it should be enough," I say, though even as I say this, I know it is unfair. You have been watching me carefully ever since we sat down. At this you lower your eyes, bringing your hand to your face and bowing your head forward. You spread your fingers as if to run them through your hair, which used to be long until a few days ago. I look down at my food and then meet your eyes again. You rub your eyebrows before dropping your hand back to the table.

"Rob," you say, something imploring in your tone. "I don't know. What if we can't make it work once I leave? Maybe this is our chance at a life together and I am ruining it."

The thought of such a thing makes me feel sick to my stomach. I don't know how long I can bear the thought of losing the one chance I have to be happy with you, so I try to push it away. I meet your eyes but not for long.

"Are we doing the wrong thing?" you question again. I look out at the pounding rain, which is hitting the ground like the downpour of questions I face.

Your voice breaks the silence once more. "Tell me what I should do."

You meet my gaze again, and I believe that you really do want me to choose for you. As if you would accept the decision I make. If I say yes to you, perhaps you would stay, I think. The words are on my tongue, but I don't say a word.

Following Your Lead

Walking down these narrow streets of Little Italy
Our shoulders and hips knock
When I look over
You are smiling
Fixated on the street musician up ahead
Playing "Volare" on the accordion
You smile more
Once you turn your head my way
I smile back, gladly pressing against you
Swept away by a sudden wave of happiness
My face stretched stupidly in a grin
As if caught in the flare of a camera flash

I have not been paying attention
To where you are leading us
I am surprised when we arrive at Petrosino Square
The little tree-filled park at the crossroads
Of the dynamic New York neighborhoods
The Bowery, Chinatown, SoHo, and Little Italy

I have been here often
I love it during the day
But at night it feels magical

You turn off the path as soon as we enter
Leading us into a section of trees and grass
That is lined with dozens of fragments of old Italian marble
Where the stones glow faintly
Under the light from the path behind
I watch as you run your hand
Down the length of one of the stones
It is a strangely sensual gesture
One that has me drawing my breath between my teeth
"Come on, Rob, you touch it too," you say

When I hesitate, you take my arm
Just above the wrist and pull it to the stone
I laugh, surrendering
Stroking it as you had done
The stone is warmer than the air
It must have soaked in the late afternoon sun
As I draw my hands away
You pull me in close
And say, "I love when you follow my lead."

Drowning in the Sea of Love

The instant I see
Your rubicund-hued smile again
My heart opens wide
To a sea of possibilities
Turning in my ribcage

There is still something about the way
Sundown kisses your eyes
But as I move closer, I see you're not alone
It's a little awkward
We look at each other almost warily
Unsure after the initial hellos
I stare at my reflection in the window behind you
I am wearing the saddest smile I have ever seen
You make polite conversation
Before introducing me to your new man
He works in finance, owns a house at the Shore
And is a New York Giants season ticket holder
Lucky guy

You have dinner reservations at Moonstruck
So you must go
My feet rock back and forth
On the wobbly wood panel below
As you lean in giving me a forced clumsy hug goodbye
I watch you turn and descend
The stairs to the street
Leaving me with the dark roar of the surf
And the dry jerking flap
Of the flag in the wind

Boundlessness

As different quadrants illuminate
I feel myself receding from the stage
From the light and sound
Of the local cover band playing there

For hours, I have managed
Not to think about you leaving
Or about the uncertainty of our future

Before we met
I never wanted permanence
Not really
I relished my freedom more
I had accepted that passionate feelings fade
All my earlier experience had confirmed it
When love that seemed certain
Simply dissolved on one side or both
Leaving little trace
But what I feel for you
Is different
It hasn't dissolved
Not even a little bit

And when you turn my shoulders to face you
Singing along with the band
These opening lines of "Yellow"
"Look at the stars,
Look how they shine for you,
And everything you do."
I want to believe
In our language of boundlessness
And the impossibility of change

September 20, 1997

I am not sure
Which memories of that day are real
And which have been stitched together
From recollections and impressions of feelings
I think I have recalled
I do remember it was a golden late September day
We both needed a break from all the city noise
So we drove down to Asbury Park
Once we arrived, we went right down to the water's edge
The sun was still mounting, and we walked
For a long while in silence
Soaking up the calming sounds of the ocean
As the chilly water continually met our bare feet
We had been walking for well over an hour
But neither of us noticed the horizon brewing
Until the weather abruptly turned icy
We looked up to see violent black clouds
Splitting the blue
The squall was on top of us in a second
As we ran up the sand, looking for cover
I turned my face to the sky
It was black, so black that our world
Was cast in the eerie glow of an eclipse
Suddenly, it became difficult
To catch my breath
I felt overcome by an overwhelming fear
The wind sang past us
Thunder shook the ground beneath us
Electricity crackled all around
You gripped me around the waist
Almost carrying me across the street
To a small motor inn
As the malevolence of panic engulfed me
You slid the motel office door open

Guiding me to a seat inside
My bottom lip quivered uncontrollably
My eyes flashed like full moons
With the dampness of imminent tears
You squatted before me
Touching my cheeks
Rubbing my shoulders
Pulling my eyes into yours
You directed my breathing
Until it was calm
And in-sync with yours
Then you did the only appropriate thing
The only Derek thing
You laughed
I smiled tentatively,
And I laughed too
With just a gesture
You had brought back the sun

Halcyon Days

The night is palpable and still
We are dressed in shorts and sweatshirts
Walking down the pier to the spot where it gets wider
Coy fireflies wink around us
I cannot stop grinning because you called
And wanted to see me again
You even put an arm around my neck
We walk in step to the gazebo and sit
I lean my head back over the rail
The sky above swims
Because I am drunk on summer
The ocean
And you
Once my head stops spinning
I see there are myriad stars
Their presence comforts me
It is relieving to see
That they are still there
Despite being perpetually outshone
By the lights of Atlantic City
You take out a Gumby PEZ dispenser
From your pocket and offer me one
I look over at you and laugh
Your thighs are twisted
Your hands dangle between your legs
I meet your eye and give you a relaxed smile
You smile back, happy
For all the emotional chaos
We have both endured since being dumped
We finally feel free
Then, bursting with idealism
You lift your chin and exclaim
"These are our halcyon days, Rob.
We must treasure each one."

AFTERWORD

When picking up a new poetry collection, a reader has several choices: Do you read it in sequence as one typically does with a novel? Do you dip around without regard for title or page number? Or do you scan the table of contents for titles that catch your attention? Some may write in the margins, star their favorite pieces, or dog-ear the pages. You may also wish to read each piece aloud as Lisa Bain recommended in her foreword. Whichever way you read this volume, I'm certain you, at bare minimum once, were transfixed in a moment of time by Robert's skillful way he can convert five seconds on a subway train beside a stranger to a reflectively vicarious, savored, relatable, experience of human connection. Any way you may approach this collection, you will be struck by a beautifully curated mixture of Robert's best poems and prose.

What is my approach to reading poetry books? I usually enjoy the "lucky dip" approach to peek around and find something that draws me in for more. I imagine a poetry collection like a buffet, I start my meal by trying a small bite of everything before loading my plate. When asked, Robert shared he approaches reading poetry books in a similar way, but no, he didn't mention anything about a buffet. The very first thing he does is read the foreword and the table of contents, then he half-haphazardly lands wherever while dog-earring, highlighting, and always writing in the margins. If he loves what he uncovers, then he will read it from beginning to end.

While Robert would say "there are no rules to reading poetry." He advises that only a few of his pieces are actually sequenced and the reader is free to jump around. He added that his idea behind the title, *kaleidoscope of colors*, is that any unique pattern of color can be found within these pages and no matter how you look at it. I will be so bold to recommend, though, that if you have only dipped around these pages or are reading this afterword first (I know there's at least one of you who has done this), then I would go back to read from the beginning. As I'm sure Lisa would agree, the flow of each of Robert's pieces in order adds to the reader's experience of this book. The reader is treated to experience the carefully interlaced emotional staging that his stand-alone pieces add around these multi-part prose stories. To this point, undoubtedly the organization of this collection has been greatly aided by Ben C. Ward's studious eye as editor, contributing to this being Robert's best work yet.

When I started reading, I read each piece one by one at a sauntering pace. I digested this collection as if it was the only thing I'd read for days so as not to miss the gems of truth woven through each entendre and raindrop scene. If you close your eyes after reading a piece like "You" or "Option B," you'll be transported to a moment of delicious relevance, even if it tastes a bit bitter. Robert has delivered profound depth in his short poems and I must say, his exceptionally crafted prose grabbed my guts the most. When read in sequence, the stories pathed throughout these pages beautifully carries you through eras and epiphanies across Robert's most vulnerable and joyous moments to date. As a tip of the hat to all the beautiful poems about Derek (more so at the end of the collection), this richness of storytelling paired with impeccable imagery could only have been done this well by Robert, our cherished "New Jersey native" ("3/18/21 Dear Derek").

This second volume of *kaleidoscope of colors* is a continuation but also a standalone piece of work. Robert says he feels his writing is more physical, honest, and intimate in this second volume. True to its name, this second volume contains threads to the first, tying us back to where we learned about Kai and continuations of memories of Derek. We get to experience the vibrant New York Robert and Derek shared together. We learn more about Robert's relationships, such as how his parents met Burt, how Robert pushed Ricardo away, and the strong bond between Kai's family and Robert. New to the reader, we are introduced to Rebecca and, with little detail given, we eagerly want to know more about her. I asked Robert, "Who is Rebecca?" He immediately laughed, sharing some stories of how they met, her renowned rooftop reveal parties, and how she embodied everything that is New York. Robert shared that he plans to add more stories of Rebecca and many of his other close friends in future books.

Robert is a master with the pen. He captures subtle experiences and displays them with impeccable narrative imagery. This is showcased in selections such as "The Cold Family Estate" and "Yellow Through the Grey" and then contrasted by "The Magic Hill" or "The Attack" with more intense experiences. Subtle or not, Robert's skillful pen continually sat me right there with him, like he did in "The Way I Look at You." There is an ease in his writing voice as he shares truths throughout. Void of pretentious riddles, it cannot be disputed that Robert gives us his honesty and vulnerability in all he writes, no matter the subject such as in "Disingenuous." Having had the privilege to get to know Robert as one of his invited poets for his anthology, *Perspective to Pen* (Cozzi & Ward, 2020), this is one of my favorite pieces in this collection because Robert gives us a glimpse of his affinity for genuine people, which I value too. His passion on the page matches the passion in his heart for human connection.

Through this collection of poems, we see Robert! His enormous heart, unwavering hopefulness, and goofy charm are on full display. Robert writes about his love for family. We get to learn more about his father, and about how special the number fifty-eight is for them. Poems share how Robert has an eye for good people at first glance, but perhaps we should say he has the heart for it ("The First Time I Saw You"). His tenacity for life and family are glaring in "Conversation with Myself." Raw or darker notes about grief ("The Tide Never Stops"), rejection ("Disdain"), mental health ("Breathing Through the Chaos"), violence ("The Attack"), and unreciprocated affection ("I Want it Back") draw us in more to the authenticity and unfiltered way Robert shares himself with the reader.

It is no secret that Robert journals in the same vein as one would devote to daily meditation or going to the gym or any daily ritual. Whatever it is that you do daily, the routine you can't live without, that's how it is with Robert and his journals. I asked him what his process is with using writings from his stacks of journals into a poetry collection ("Fifty Years"). Much to my pleasure for guessing correctly, he shared that when he wants to write about something, he grabs the details from an entry and then builds around that to create a detailed poem but with more poetic flavor than was in the journal entry. I imagined this is how he wrote "September 20, 1997." No wonder his poems are packed with details that one may think only a photograph could recall. If he was sitting here, I'm sure he'd be playfully encouraging you to write in a journal too. This collection lets us reflect on what's most important in the world through Robert's eyes. Truly, we see how genuine human connection (and maybe great food and music, too) are most valuable for him. He cherishes friends like no other. Three years after releasing volume one, which was dedicated to Jerome, Robert laments in his piece "February 17th." Sharing so much of himself in his work, we get to learn of the people in Robert's life that have made an impact on who he is, including bonds that continue despite the grave, which is remarkably inspiring. He can relate to anyone without the added lens of society's bias, one of the many reasons I love Robert and his work. Hitting on so many aspects of human connection, "Holding on Together" is one of his most inspiring poems in this collection that can anchor each of us in our busy lives to slow down and "share time" with one another. But don't be mistaken by so many of these tender moments, just when the reader gets used to narration of love, Robert cheekily throws a curveball to remind us about how temporary these moments can be. Flipping the switch again, he brings us back with a line, like in "The Train Back to New Jersey," he wrote, "I look at you for a long time/ And think about how I could make a whole life / Out of these moments."

The stories Robert shares with us are beyond captivating. He included several multi-part poems that he reveals to the reader in a variety of ways (e.g., using dates, "the day after," or the easy-to-notice Part 1, 2, 3 etc.) The nostalgic notes he brings with mentions of M&Ms, Stevie Nicks, The Beatles, Rolling Rock beer, and the roller rink (to name a few), sprinkles playfulness and vibrance to this collection. This leaves me wondering, why doesn't Robert write a novel or screenplay? After reading all three parts of "Pink Champagne," I think you'll ask the same question. Of course, I had to ask him, and you'll be pleased to hear that Robert has been experimenting with fellow poets on different styles of story writing, which he shares on his Instagram page. Perhaps we will get to see some different writing formats from Robert published in the future. Mark these words, folks! (Well, I suppose I just did.)

Even as a forty-year-old sassy poet from Canada, I can relate to many of the treasures within Robert's work. What Robert loves about "Whitman at 3am" is what I love about Robert. The feelings he brings about as well as the deep reflections are a gift to an open mind. He has made me think of blissful ignorance or deceit in different ways. That, in a matter-of-fact way, these experiences are just a part of life and it's how things go sometimes. I can't recall ever feeling anger from Robert's words. But don't mistake this for him being without a backbone, as he is one of the kindest yet steadfast people I know. He also provides us a fresh appreciation for unconventional beauty and "old souls" in many of his poems. Didn't he make you appreciate your own partner more or, if not, make you wish to be with someone who makes you feel like his dinner partner made him feel in "The Diner's Remedy?"

If you highlighted your favorite pieces, did you also pick "You" or "Just What I Didn't Want to Hear?" If you felt a longing for the ocean while reading, did you also note other things you wish to experience? After reading this collection, I definitely want to sit by the sea with my eyes closed again soon, taste a "Baked by Melissa" peanut butter cupcake for the first time, fall asleep on the beach nestled into my lover's chest, and roller skate backwards at Roxy (and if time travel were possible, I'd wish to go back in time to go there with Robert and Derek). When you are feeling low, remember how Robert's words made you feel and reread your favorite pieces and your list of things you want to experience too.

When you close this book and walk away from the pages, let Robert's experiences linger in how you view the people around you. See the rich colors of us all like he has done when immortalizing a stranger from ten seconds on a train in "Missed Opportunity." His narrative brings you right to the moments he's describing. You are there, too. You feel what he feels and are at the mercy of sharp turns away from golds and oranges toward the darker hues of blue. My heart leaped and broke over and over throughout these pages. To feel the intensity that Robert lives his life is truly a gift that invigorates, if you let it, and brings the beauty of human connection to any story you could tell. On life's stage, the spotlight falls where it may, but Robert will turn on the flood lights so as not to miss the love, loss, desire, and playful experiences happening all around us.

After all of Robert's words, and mine, who do you want to reach out to? Is there anyone you are thinking of now? Any you think would be open to you sending a message? Any you think would be eager to walk together so your "shoulders and hips knock" ("Following Your Lead")? Perhaps you are thinking of a time you first made eye contact with someone? Or of a time your fingers brushed with someone? That's the effect Robert left with me. Even if I haven't experienced a quarter of the things he has, I feel like if I did experience those things, I wouldn't miss any morsel of it. Because if I've learned anything at all from being Robert's friend, solidified by this book, is that silence is where the magic happens—listen for it, look for it, and when it happens—write about it to find truthful treasures.

To close, I'm leaving you with a quote from "The Goodbye" to say, "'this is only goodbye for now.'" Goodbye is easy, knowing the stories will keep coming and there will be no shortage of pages. We didn't find it hard to love you, Robert, we really didn't.

-Emily Salt

ACKNOWLEDGMENTS

I would like to express my thanks to Annemarie Biondi, Andy O'Hara, Lisa Bain, Brian Fuchs, Shanika Benoit, Max Asbeek Brusse, Cody James, Emily Salt, Nathaniel Chin, Anthony James Rivera, Davian Williams, Carl Strout-Collard, Donna Catanzaro, Nick Niscelli, Nicholas Niscelli, Michael Lidoski, Pete Donatelli, Matthew Ryan Woolfrey, Paul Kocum, Ed Burgos, Loretta Obstfeld, Gabriela Parraga, Karen Dinsmore, Jaime Schneider, Glenn Randall, Nathan Higham, Joe Nix, Jason Fitzgerald, Duke Al, Emily Willard, the Instagram poetry community, my library kids, Sandy Iammatteo, Bryan Glenn, Pete Donatelli, Ricardo Ramierez, Burt Conners, Christian Sonnets, Jo Ann Carra, Jim Kurzawa, Kailin Alfaro, Jorge Alarcon, Mary Healy-Davis, Gerard Yatcilla, Luke Emsley, Atlas W. Keating, Rhiannon Marie, Kindra M. Austin, Alex Gonzalez, Rowanne Carberry, Lindy Van Hillo, and my Instagram and Facebook followers and friends.

Note

Two poems in this collection have been previously published elsewhere: "The Sound Heard Above the City" (*Perspective to Pen: An Anthology*), and "Ode to Sal Mineo" (Scissortail Quarterly #3).

You can find Robert at his:

Instagram: @robertcozziauthor
Twitter: @RobertACozzi1
Website: www. robertcozziauthor.com

About the Author

Raised in Westfield, New Jersey, Robert A. Cozzi has published six books of poetry and an anthology, as well as written plays and short stories. He has won six eLit awards for his collections *Blanket of Hearts* (2016), *Sky of Dreams* (2017), *kaleidoscope of colors* (2019), and *Perspective to Pen: An Anthology* (2020). He lives and works in Basking Ridge, New Jersey, never too far from his blanket of hearts or his copy of *On the Road*. Look forward to his upcoming release, *Two Kinds of Love*, later this year.

Made in the USA
Middletown, DE
15 July 2021

44031848R00188